ANGER MANAGEMENT

Do you work with angry children?
Are you wondering why young people don't listen when they are angry?
Are you exhausted from trying to understand angry behaviour?

Anger Management is a practical guide that will help you to stay calm in the face of angry outbursts from children and young people. Written by chartered psychologists with extensive experience in the field, this helpful book will:

- increase your understanding of anger
- offer you a range of practical management interventions
- help you to manage your own behaviours to build more effective relationships
- reduce the stress experienced by staff and parents who lack confidence in the face of aggressive behaviour.

With stress and anger levels amongst young people at an all time high, this second edition of *Anger Management* is particularly timely. It reflects the significant developments in the field of neuro-psychology and our understanding of the physiology of emotions. It also identifies the significant changes in legislation and guidance that have taken place in education and health and social care over the last decade and explores the implications of these changes for practitioners.

Containing information, explanations and practical advice that will enable you to cope with angry behaviour in the best way possible, as well as a range of helpful photocopiable resources, this book will prove invaluable to teachers as well as parents, carers, psychologists, social workers and health care workers.

Adrian Faupel is Professional and Academic Tutor to the Doctorate in Educational Psychology at the University of Southampton, UK.

Elizabeth Herrick is a Consultant Psychologist for Children's Services in Southampton Local Authority, UK.

Peter Sharp is Chief Executive at the Centre for Workforce Intelligence (Department of Health) and Director of Learning and Well-being at Mouchel Management and Consulting, UK.

D1218161

ANGER MANAGEMENT

A practical guide

Second edition

Adrian Faupel, Elizabeth Herrick and Peter Sharp

Routledge
Taylor & Francis Group

LONDON AND NEW YORK

First edition published 1998
by Routledge
This edition published 2011
by Routledge
2 Park Square, Milton Park, Abingdon, Oxon, OX14 4RN

Simultaneously published in the USA and Canada
by Routledge
270 Madison Avenue, New York, NY 10016

Routledge is an imprint of the Taylor & Francis Group, an informa business

Typeset in Helvetica Neue by FiSH Books
Printed and bound in Great Britain by The MPG Books Group

British Library Cataloguing in Publication Data
A catalogue record for this book is available from the British Library

Library of Congress Cataloging-in-Publication Data
Faupel, Adrian.
   Anger management : a practical guide / Adrian Faupel, Elizabeth Herrick and Peter Sharp. – 2nd ed.
      p. cm.
   1. Anger. 2. Anger in children. I. Herrick, Elizabeth. II. Sharp, Peter, 1955- III. Title.
   BF575.A5F38 2011
   152.4'7–dc22   2010018658

ISBN13: 978-0-415-58071-7 (pbk)
ISBN13: 978-0-203-83988-1 (ebk)

CONTENTS

List of figures   vii
Acknowledgments   viii
Preface   ix

Part 1: What do we mean by anger?   1

1   Introduction   2

2   Perspectives on anger   10

3   What does anger do to you?   18

4   What do we do with anger?   25

Part 2: Planning to avoid the storm   33

5   Managing systems   34

6   Managing ourselves   43

7   Managing children and young people   49

Part 3: The fireworks   55

8   Working with angry children   57

9   The explosion   68

10 The aftermath   76

Part 4: Practical applications   85

11 Help for parents and carers   86

Part 5: Appendices   **91**

Appendix 1: Observation checklist: Primary (5–11)   92

Appendix 2: Observation checklist: Secondary (11–16)   93

Appendix 3: Anger thermometer   94

Appendix 4: Anger log   95

Appendix 5: Anger triggers   96

Appendix 6: What makes me angry?   97

Appendix 7: What do I think?   98

Appendix 8: How do I feel?   100

Appendix 9: Keeping calm   101

Appendix 10: Drawing the feelings in my body   103

Appendix 11: Developing a solution   104

Appendix 12: A solution-focused interview with a young person prone to angry
            outbursts   107

Appendix 13: The beginnings of change   109

Appendix 14: Effective anger   110

Appendix 15: Tips for parents of toddlers   112

Appendix 16: Tips for parents of primary age children   114

Appendix 17: Tips for parents of teenagers   116

Appendix 18: What children and teachers say about anger   118

Bibliography   124
Index   127

LIST OF FIGURES

Part 1

1.1	The five dimensions of emotional literacy	3
1.2	The firework model	5
1.3	The assault cycle	6
1.4	Overall plan of managing anger	7
1.5	'The storm'	8
2.1	The behaviourist approach to the relationships between behaviour, thinking and feeling	10
2.2	Exemplifying a psychodynamic view of the relationships between feeling, thinking and behaviour	12
2.3	Exemplifying a more cognitive-behavioural view of the relationships between thinking, feeling and behaviour	13
3.1	The anger pie	19

Part 2

	Planning to avoid the storm	33
5.1	Bronfenbrenner's ecological model of development	34
5.2	Promoting school effectiveness based on the Bronfenbrenner model	35
5.3	Three levels of intervention in anger management	35

Part 3

	Defusing the firework	55
8.1	Early warning signs	59
8.2	Protecting against the possibility of storm damage	61
9.1	Dealing with the explosion	68
9.2	The firework explodes	69
9.3	The crisis phase	70
10.1	The aftermath	76
10.2	Quiet reflections	84

ACKNOWLEDGMENTS

The authors wish to express sincere appreciation to their educational psychologist colleagues, particularly in Southampton and Hampshire, for their ideas and support over many years, and to the many teachers, other adults and pupils with whom they have worked in struggling with issues of anger and aggression in schools and in the community.

Our personal thanks go to our partners and families: warm thanks from Adrian to Diane Solecki and young Simon; from Liz Herrick to Rick Brown; and from Peter Sharp to Lindsey, Chloe and Poppy Sharp. Your support and encouragement has been a great help – and we are continuing to try to manage our own anger more effectively.

Adrian Faupel
Liz Herrick
Peter Sharp

PREFACE

Political context

Since the first edition of this book in 1998, the context for this work has changed considerably with legislation (Children Act 2004) focusing national awareness around the maxim: *Every Child Matters* (DfES, 2005).

Every Child Matters (ECM) is recognition of the importance of the well-being of each and every child, and that all practices should therefore be about 'change for children'. The five key outcomes that all authorities are now legally obliged to focus on are:

- physical and mental health ('being healthy');
- protection from harm and neglect ('staying safe');
- education and training ('enjoying and achieving');
- contributing to society ('making a positive contribution');
- social and economic well-being ('good start and secure employment').

The roots of this Act can be traced to the Victoria Climbié Inquiry (House of Commons Health Committee, 2003) that led directly to the government's acceptance of a number of recommendations (Laming Report, 2009) on how to prevent further tragic loss of life by more integrated working practices involving all responsible adults caring for children.

There have, therefore, been significant structural and policy changes, both nationally and locally. Nationally, until the new coalition government came to power in 2010 the Department for Education and Schools and the Department for Health and Social Care were combined to form a single Department for Children, Schools and Families. Locally (within local authorities and primary health care trusts), services for children have been combined into a single Children's Trust to oversee the direction of local policy and practice. The trust board comprises representatives from all services working with children in each locality.

In practice, this has led to education, health and social care services working together in multi-agency teams structured around children and families and delivering within the community rather than based centrally.

A number of other initiatives support more integrated, standardised services for children, both within localities and across the UK. These have been developed with the intention of improving services to avoid duplication, repetition, gaps and postcode lotteries of provision. These include:

- The Common Assessment Framework (CAF);
- The Lead Professional role (LP);
- The Children's Workforce Development Council (CWDC);
- Sure Start and Children's centres.

The Common Assessment Framework (CAF) has been developed to ensure early intervention and prevention within universal service provision. It was designed to be used with children causing concern, for whom early intervention could prevent the necessity later of more expensive and intensive specialist provision or of their slipping through the net completely. This framework provides a standardised assessment so that *all* children are able to have access to the same range of services irrespective of where they live. It also provides a robust assessment model and an effective tool for supporting integrated multi-agency working at all levels of need.

The Lead Professional role, (LP), is carried out by an individual identified as one person who can provide a single point of contact for parents, young people, practitioners and professionals. The LP is also responsible for co-ordinating and monitoring service provision for children and their families. This role should alleviate the problem of families not knowing which agency to talk to when needing ongoing support, and should speed up access to appropriate provision.

The Children's Workforce Development Council has been established to ensure that all practitioners working with children have achieved a minimal level of training about safeguarding children and about child development. This is to ensure that all those professionals have at least basic skills and awareness of how to protect and support children and their families.

The Sure Start initiative is funded nationally and is intended to support children under 5 and their families, particularly in deprived areas of the country. As this is considered to be a very successful model, it has subsequently been extended to incorporate a more general model of support for the under 5s that focuses on providing services within the local community. Children's centres have been developed across the country to enable families to access support within their local communities. A range of provision is available within the children's centres as well as more informal opportunities for building local networks of support.

The principles underpinning these initiatives include:

- identifying and addressing needs that are particular to a specific geographical area;
- prevention and early identification of difficulties;
- services being made available within local communities;
- avoiding complicated referral systems;
- having provision that is more accessible geographically;
- having a range of professionals/practitioners working primarily in one area to enable integrated working on a formal and informal basis;
- providing a meeting place for parents to encourage parents to establish their own support networks.

More recent initiatives that have major implications for improving services for children and young people within the five domains identified in the *Every Child Matters* agenda include:

* *The Steer Report: Learning Behaviour* (Steer, 2005 and 2009);
* *Your Child, Your Schools, Our Future* (DCSF, 2009);
* *A Good Childhood* (Layard and Dunn, 2009).

The Steer Report

Within educational settings there has been debate about the extent to which schools and colleges should be managing and supporting children and young people with their emotional and social development as well as expecting high academic attainments. It is generally accepted that the two are inextricably linked but less clear how we manage the tensions that arise between them both politically and professionally. The Steer Commission was set up by the government as a response to the increasing concerns over the deterioration of behaviour, particularly in secondary schools. The report, *Learning Behaviour: Lessons Learned* (Steer, 2009) places a responsibility on children's trusts to identify how they will deliver the full range of mental health and psychological well-being services across the full spectrum of need. The report also puts an emphasis on improving both initial teacher training and ongoing professional development for all those working within education. It suggests that a school with exceptional success in behaviour management could apply to become a training school. Other initiatives suggested within the report include:

* the development of learning mentors for young people;
* parent support advisers to support the relationship between home and school;
* parenting practitioners to provide parenting programmes.

Building Britain's future

A recent White Paper from the DCSF, *Your Child, Your Schools, Our Future: Building a 21st-century Schools System* (DCSF, 2009), reinforces the views that children and young people will need to develop new skills in order to meet the challenging demands of the future. Young people will need to be flexible, to manage change, to take responsibility for themselves, including their health, and to contribute to the development of a sustainable environment. It also places a high level of importance on establishing 'good behaviour, strong discipline, order and safety in schools'.

A Good Childhood

This report was commissioned by the National Children's Society to provide up-to-date evidence of children's views about their own experiences within childhood. The findings suggested that there are still marked differences in outcomes for children in educational, health and economic achievements, and that these are dependent upon the areas in which they live, with the worst outcomes being seen in the most deprived areas of the UK. Amongst the various contributing factors identified were a perceived lack of discipline within schools and the community generally. This was seen to have significant influence on children's behaviour and experiences. Deliberate disruption, destructive behaviours and bullying were identified as increasing issues of concern.

The report notes that one in five, 5–16-year-olds present with significant mental health difficulties ranging from anxiety and depression to challenging and destructive behaviours. Only a quarter of these children receive any specialist help. Anger can often be seen as the most challenging of the emotions as, when expressed inappropriately, it can lead to extremely challenging behaviours that threaten mental health and emotional well-being, good order and safety for the individual concerned and those around them.

It is our belief that increasing the abilities of *all* those working with children to feel competent and confident in supporting children with emotional and social difficulties enables them to provide early and effective intervention and so prevent mild and moderate difficulties escalating into more serious mental health problems. This book provides insight and skills for professionals, practitioners, parents and carers in supporting our children and young people in this way.

Professional context

Improving mental health has long been recognised by psychologists as a valuable factor in contributing to individual health and well-being, and social harmony.

Emotional well-being

In addition to the *ECM* agenda, there has been a growing interest in promoting emotional well-being in all areas of life. In our first edition, 'emotional literacy' was defined as the ability to recognise, understand, handle and appropriately express emotions (Faupel *et al.*, 1998), and work to promote emotional literacy was undertaken by the authors with staff from over 60 local authorities across Britain. Anger management is one facet of the promotion of emotional literacy and has direct links to all five of the *ECM* outcomes set out above.

The DfES materials for the development of social and emotional aspects of learning are part of both the primary and secondary strategies. This SEAL (DCSF, 2005) initiative has been developed over the last decade, and two of the authors (Sharp and Faupel) were members of the former DfES advisory group on social, emotional and behavioural skills. The underlying concerns about increasingly disruptive and aggressive behaviour mean that anger management has become a key area for teachers, learning support assistants, parents and professionals to develop approaches to enhance the social and emotional aspects of learning and well-being.

The content of the first edition of this book has been used for:

- developing anger management groups with children and young people (Sharp and Herrick, 2000);
- training and development workshops for teachers, learning support assistants and parents;

- other forms of developmental group work, e.g. self-esteem, social skills and managing conflict;
- developing practical resources for understanding and teaching social and emotional development (cf. Faupel, 2003 and Woodcock, in press);
- informing aspects of the development of Social and Emotional Aspects of Learning (SEAL) and Social, Emotional and Behavioural Skills (SEBS), which are now part of the primary and Key Stage 3 national strategies.

Early evaluation of these national programmes suggests that they are beginning to influence teacher practice, and particularly in focusing on whole-school issues and the 'whole child'. Anger management is just one important aspect of the emotional literacy agenda (incorporating SEAL and SEBS), and is also a feature of the National Healthy Schools Programme (NHSP).

The feedback from readers and recipients of training from the authors leads us to believe that the ideas in this book are robust, reliable and useful. If 'what matters is what works', then teachers, learning support assistants, other professionals, children and young people, and parents have all assured us that this works well for them.

Other local authorities around the UK have used this work as a starting point for their own development work within the domain of emotional development. The authors have been involved in working with many services, both nationally and internationally, to further the development of emotional and behavioural development. This work soon moved from being a tool for working with children with difficulties to being much more appropriately applied to all pupils and adults. Effective management of emotions is a necessary part of growing and developing as an effective human being. It was this that led Southampton LEA in 1998 to establish emotional literacy as an equal priority with literacy and numeracy as a city-wide initiative.

Since the first edition, we have been able to extend our practice beyond the field of education to include other agencies, by working in multi-agency settings with children, young people and parents. In working with teams of professionals and practitioners around specific children and young people's needs, it has become apparent that the ideas and practical application developed within this book have a wider relevance for all those working within children's trusts and primary care trusts. Feedback has also been received from practitioners working with adults; for example, within parenting programmes and work in prisons.

Finally...

It can be seen from the above changes in political thinking that the expectations of adults working with children and young people have risen significantly, whilst the expectations of the young people themselves are going to increase as competition for decreased resources continues. These initiatives provide an expectation that there will be a wide range of practitioners working to provide early intervention and preventative services for children and families. They will also be expected to have a higher level of knowledge and skills than was previously the case, including a basic understanding of how to manage emotions.

There have also been significant developments in our academic understanding of neuro-physiology, neuropsychology, the nature of emotions and feelings, and the importance of attachment theory and emotional regulation to underlying aggression. This, together with the above changes in political direction and combined with the ongoing experience of the authors in the field of emotional well-being, has contributed to the importance of developing a second edition of this book. The authors anticipate that the content of this updated edition will provide a valuable resource to support all practitioners working with children and families, as well as to empower parents to understand their own and their children's behaviours, and the emotional needs underpinning them.

PART 1

What do we mean by anger?

Chapter 1

INTRODUCTION

I get angry when I want to,
I get angry when I don't,
I'll get angry when I'll try to,
I'll get angry when I won't.

I get angry when I'm threatened,
I get angry when I'm sad,
but I get angry when I'm happy,
and that just makes me mad!

Anger is a good thing,
and then again it's bad,
so now we've got it sorted,
I'm really feeling glad.

Within the programme for developing social and emotional aspects of learning there are five key domains (Goleman, 1996) see Figure 1.1.

Anger management has links to all of the five domains, but of all the domains, this book focuses particularly on the development of skills and strategies to manage feelings, and especially feelings associated with problem anger.

Anger engenders mixed emotions. It often leaves us feeling wrecked, or racked with guilt. There is a view that to optimise emotional well-being we must express a whole range of feelings, but that anger is potentially our most dangerous emotion and, at its most extreme, can lead to death. Contrast this with Freud's view that unexpressed anger actually causes depression and it becomes clear that the contradictions in the poem above are very real for us all.

So what is anger?

When anger is defined as 'extreme displeasure' (*Concise Oxford Dictionary*), it fails to convey the full force of the effects of anger, both on the person being angry and on anyone on the receiving end of the anger, or merely witnessing it as a passive observer. To compound the confusion, anger is taken to be an emotion, and hence is further defined by the *Oxford Dictionary* as an 'instinctive feeling as opposed to reason'. Add to this a widely held view that anger is a negative emotion and it is perhaps easy to see why

Self-awareness	Managing feelings	Motivation	Empathy	Social skills
• Observing yourself • Recognising feelings • Building a vocabulary • Relationship between thoughts, feelings and actions • Recognition of patterns of feelings • Self-appraisal	• Handling feelings • What's behind a feeling? • Responding to others • Finding ways to handle fears and anxiety • Resilience • Using intuition • Manage stress • Manage energy	• Understanding goals • Choosing goals • Planning steps to target • Overcoming obstacles • Persevering • Deferred gratification	• Observe and recognise others' feelings • Understand others' feelings • Respect others' perspective • Appreciate differences • Communicate warmth re. others' feelings	• Talk about feelings effectively • Be a good listener • Send 'I' messages • Negotiate with others • Make use of mediation • Respectful confrontation • Apologise and make amends • Sensitive feedback

Figure 1.1 The five dimensions of emotional literacy (after Goleman, 1996)

children may be bewildered by adult reactions to their anger, which are usually to extinguish it, or to punish them for having the feeling in the first place.

Anger and our basic human needs

In this book we are making a distinction between emotions and feelings (see Chapter 2). Anger can be thought of as a feeling that may arise from a primary emotion such as fear. Fear may, in turn, be bound up with embarrassment, disappointment, injury, exploitation, envy or loss. All of these feelings represent a threat of some kind, though we often don't recognise this while angry. They can be interpreted as a threat to our 'belonging', which is being increasingly recognised, since Abraham Maslow's (1943, 1968) work, as being our fundamental human need. The importance of identifying basic human needs that are not being met was also a building-block of William Glasser's (1986) choice theory discussed further in Chapter 8.

Children may demonstrate inappropriate behaviours in an attempt to get their needs met if they have not learnt how to do so effectively. In turn, children who have little or no anger control are less likely to meet these needs without violating the best interests of others.

Beyond the needs outlined above are 'higher-level' needs as described by Abraham Maslow (1968). Specifically, these include ego needs, which encompass self-respect, self-confidence, achievement and competence. At the top of Maslow's hierarchy is self-actualisation, which occurs when a person realises his or her full potential, a relatively rare phenomenon. For very angry children, the reality is that Maslow's 'lower-level' needs are the likely focus for any support work offered by responsible adults, including parents, carers, teachers and other professionals. These needs include:

- physical – air, food, rest, shelter;
- safety – protection against danger, threat, deprivation, freedom from fear;
- social – belonging, association, acceptance, giving and receiving love and friendship.

Maslow's hierarchy has been related to a hierarchy of emotional motivators (Zohar and Marshall, 2004). It is not appropriate to examine this theory in detail in this book, but it is helpful to see how it might help us to understand children's behaviour when their needs have not been met. Maslow's 'lower-level' needs are described, by him, as deficiency needs. Zohar and Marshall's motivators that are associated with these include:

- guilt;
- fear;
- anger.

Sadly, there are significant numbers of children who are so troubled that immediate support and direction may be necessary to ensure their own safety or the safety of others. The necessarily intrusive management of behaviour in these circumstances is described in the context of crisis management in Chapter 9, The explosion. Such reactive strategies designed to manage dangerous behaviour are only acceptable as a short-term expedient and should be a prelude to moving children on to becoming more receptive to understanding and helping themselves.

When anger becomes significantly disruptive in a child's life, it may lead to mild, moderate or severe difficulties in managing their emotional and social life, This, in turn, could escalate into mental health problems over time, which could affect all of the outcomes identified within the *Every Child Matters* (DfES, 2005) agenda, i.e. health, safety, educational and vocational achievement, economic well-being and participation in community. This is likely to persist through adulthood unless support is offered and accepted. This inability to manage emotions will frequently manifest itself in adult life as one of the factors contributing to a failure to form or sustain meaningful relationships, and at worst may lead to a vicious circle involving violence to self or others.

Anger will also be considered as a reflection of emotional difficulties that may lead to, or arise from, emotional disorder, e.g. attachment disorder. For children, the roots of such disorder are often known to teachers, parents, carers and others, but less frequently do they receive a planned and sophisticated response. Institutionally, we have become increasingly adept at identifying, assessing and responding to academic learning difficulties but are far less adept at doing the same for social, emotional or behavioural difficulties.

Finally, anger will be considered as an instrumental behaviour that achieves particular outcomes and may be part of what some writers describe as conduct disorder. It can be seen as attention-seeking behaviour, or perhaps better described as attention-*needing* behaviour, since the anger expressed is usually a result of a lack of positive attention in a child's formative years.

So anger will be considered an essential part of being human, and accepted as having an evolutionary or adaptive significance, and a recognition, too, that anger can be either useful and positive, or harmful and negative. Aristotle's challenge, as described in Daniel Goleman's book *Emotional Intelligence* (1996), perfectly describes this perplexing and fundamental dichotomy:

> *Anyone can become angry – that is easy. But to be angry with the right person, to the right degree, at the right time, for the right purpose, and in the right way – this is not easy.*
>
> (Aristotle, *The Nicomachean Ethics*, cited in Goleman, 1996)

Aristotle's challenge is to manage our emotional life with intelligence, and Goleman eloquently argues that 'we have gone too far in emphasising the value and import of the purely rational – what IQ measures – in human life. Intelligence can come to nothing when emotions hold sway.' Whilst one angry child may resemble another at the level of physiological response, the way in which each adapts to and controls their feelings of rage differs widely according to the level of skills in the other domains, as identified above. This, in turn, will be affected by upbringing and personal traits. This means there is interaction between inherited and acquired characteristics, and we can certainly influence behaviour through teaching and learning. Currently, still too little work is done with parents to make them more effective in nurturing emotional development, and, arguably, even less with teachers to help them in their work with children. We have highlighted the very important recent developments in developing a curriculum for emotional well-being, and this book seeks to offer advice and guidance to professionals and practitioners working with children and young people as well as parents and other readers who are interested in managing anger effectively both for themselves and others.

Anger as a firework

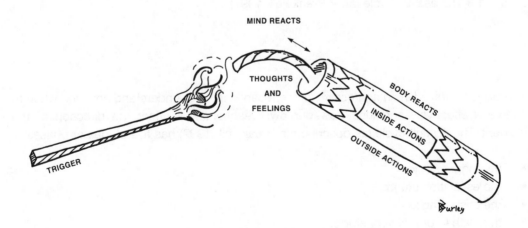

Figure 1.2 The firework model (after Novaco)

Figure 1.2 is a useful model for understanding anger. It is adapted from Novaco's Model for Anger Arousal (in Feindler and Ecton, 1986). The firework model has proven particularly accessible and memorable to young children, adolescents and, indeed, the adults that we have worked with in running anger management groups over many years.

When presented with a three-dimensional representation of the firework model, even quite young children seem able to grasp the notion of either avoiding matches or triggers (such as people, situations, times, words), or else minimising or reducing their impact, by being able to rethink or reframe their reaction to the triggers, and either lengthen their fuse or extinguish it before exploding! Later in the book we will return to show how this model may be used to support anger management group work with children and young people.

The assault cycle

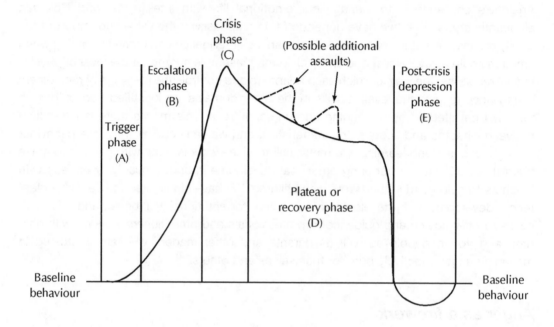

Figure 1.3 The assault cycle (after Breakwell, 1997)

The stages involved in an aggressive incident can help us to understand how and when to intervene effectively and also how our own reactions will affect the direction of the incident. The assault cycle (as described in Breakwell, 1997) has five stages or phases:

- the trigger stage;
- the escalation stage;
- the crisis stage;
- the plateau or recovery stage;
- the post-crisis depression stage.

The trigger stage can be related to the firework model, and is an event that 'ignites' a person's fuse, stimulating thoughts and feelings that lead to problem anger. It is the stage at which a pupil perceives, imagines or remembers an incident or event as threatening.

The escalation stage is the time at which the body is preparing itself physiologically for 'fight or flight'. When under attack, we share the same mechanisms as lower animals, using parts and functions of our brain that we have inherited from our biological ancestors. To prepare the body for violent action, either to fight or to flee, adrenalin is released into the body, the muscles tense, breathing becomes rapid and blood pressure rises.

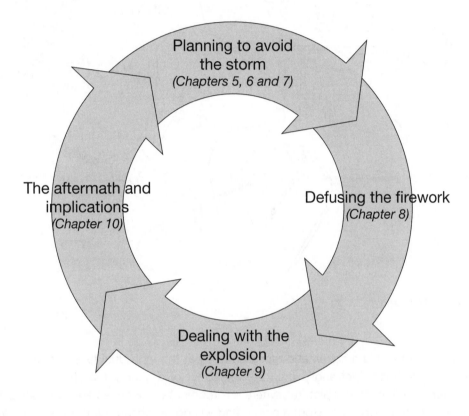

Figure 1.4 The overall plan for managing anger

These two stages will be looked at in more detail in Part 3, Chapter 8, 'Working with angry children'. The crisis stage is when the pupil is so aroused as to be completely unable to make rational judgements or to demonstrate any empathy with others. The post-crisis/depression stage is the phase in which the body needs to rest and recover from the high state of arousal that it has been in.

Anger as a storm

Figure 1.5 'The storm'

If the firework model is a schematic representation at the individual level, showing what happens to me when I get angry, then the metaphor of a 'storm' may help to describe anger in terms of the 'bigger picture', where environmental influences are as important as the reaction of the individual. Storms occur, and will go on occurring, but there are ways to avoid storms or to minimise their impact, and certainly to weather them and deal with any aftermath.

Some meteorological storms are heralded by well-understood indicators, such as gathering clouds and changes in pressure or wind direction, light fading or sudden darkness. So it is with some emotional outbursts or violent incidents; teachers often report that they know what kind of a day a class or pupil are going to have simply from such matters as the way the pupils enter a room first thing in the morning. Clearly, then, avoidance strategies will be of great help in trying to head off a storm, or go round it rather than through it. We will look more closely at planning to avoid a storm, including assessing risk, in Part 2, Chapters 5–7.

Even with superlative planning, it will not always be possible to ward off angry outbursts. It is then useful to return to the firework model and see what we can do to help children/ young people to avoid lit matches and to defuse, or at least lengthen, the fuse. This will be explored in Chapter 8, 'Working with angry children'.

In Chapter 9, 'The explosion', we acknowledge that we cannot get it right all the time, especially if the anger is made less predictable by drugs, alcohol or psychosis. Some explosions appear to be 'unannounced' and adults will sometimes describe children's anger as appearing 'out of the blue' which is our everyday expression for the storm metaphor. Here the emphasis must be on managing the crisis or explosion and on the strategies that practitioners and parents might include to defuse the anger before it becomes dangerous, so reducing the risk of danger to self and others at that time.

Strategies for clearing up after the storm or explosion, and making sure all involved learn from the experience and plan to reduce the likelihood of a similar 'disaster' happening, will be explored in Chapter 10, 'The aftermath'.

A range of methods of supporting children and young people in changing their behaviour will be considered within each of the chapters in Parts 2 and 3. Specific advice for parents and carers is offered in Part 4, though we hope parents will be encouraged to read the rest of the book by what they find there.

For readers intending to use the book as a source for running groups or working with individual children, or for teaching, coaching, advising and direct support, the appendices are available as a photocopiable resource, and we would highly recommend 'Group work with angry children' (Woodcock, in press) as a more comprehensive resource.

Chapter 2

PERSPECTIVES ON ANGER

To understand and to manage anger is no easy task as it involves a complex interaction of thoughts, feelings, behaviour and physiology. There is increasing recognition of the importance of physiology in our understanding of emotions and feelings. In fact, neuro-psychologists are making clearer distinctions between emotions (which are bodily states) and feelings (which are mental states). Antonio Damasio (2003) suggests that 'Emotions play out in the theatre of the body. Feelings play out in the theatre of the mind.'

Actions and behaviour carried out in the heat of anger cause damage to one's self and to others, so it becomes essential to understand what causes or influences that behaviour. Behaviour both includes the suppression of anger, which can be harmful to one's self, and the overt expression of anger which can be harmful to others. This is further explained in Chapter 4: 'What do we do with anger?'

There is concern not only about the increasing levels of violence by children and young people that is done to others, but also about increasing rates of depression and self-harm (Layard and Dunn, 2009). The latter may well reflect anger being internalised and finding expression in harm to the self.

The firework model, described in Chapter 1, is a simple and effective way to understand what happens when people get angry, but a deeper understanding of the related issues will be obtained by considering a wider range of perspectives.

Psychologists have differed in the ways they have seen the three components – thinking, feeling and behaviour – interacting, and this has influenced the way they have seen how such behaviour should be managed or controlled. The following accounts are necessarily somewhat oversimplified, but they at least reflect the relative emphasis that psychologists have given to each of the three components.

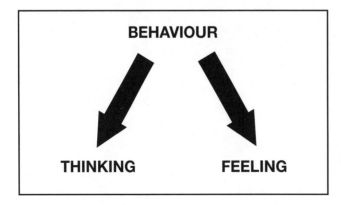

Figure 2.1 The behaviourist approach to the relationships between behaviour, thinking and feeling

The behaviourist approach sees 'behaviour' as primary (Figure 2.1). It is the way we behave that really matters. Behaviourists believe that behaviour is controlled by the past history of rewards and punishments given to particular behaviour. As a general rule, there is a greater probability of a child hitting another child if on a previous occasion the child with the sweets has complied with the demand to hand over his sweets. Behaviour that is followed by an aversive consequence is less likely to be repeated.

Another way of viewing the likelihood of behaviour occurring is the 'ABC model', which is frequently used as a behaviour management tool in schools. Technically, this is known as the 'functional analysis of behaviour' for it sees behaviour (B) as a function of the antecedents (A) and the consequences (C). This means that if either the antecedents of the behaviour or its consequences, or both, are changed, the probability of that behaviour happening will also be changed. The antecedents are particularly important in preventative aspects of controlling difficult behaviour. The general context, or even the specific triggers provoking anger, can be such things as irritants (noise, overcrowding, heat etc.), and these are clearly environmental aspects that can often be changed. Other antecedents are to do with the way demands are made of people – for example, the way a teacher tells a pupil off can 'provoke' an angry reaction. Another teacher, with a different style, achieves the same compliance, but without cornering the pupil. So the differing ways demands or requests are made to pupils can provoke different reactions. Whole-school policies also fit into this antecedent framework – schools which have very clearly articulated boundaries of what is acceptable behaviour and what is not, and which focus on teaching new, more acceptable, behaviours, consistently seem to experience less abusive and aggressive behaviour. Schools that have an ethos reflecting an underlying belief that the 'sort of children we have here' frequently get into fights, and so don't bother to do much about it when that happens, are more likely to have pupils displaying anger and aggressive behaviour.

The behaviourist view is not that pupils who show frequent and aggressive anger are simply born that way, but that they have learnt to be the way they are by being rewarded in some way when they have displayed anger. 'I get what I want as soon as I throw a temper tantrum' is a lesson learnt when people give in to the temper tantrum. Angry people have, generally, very low frustration tolerance – they cope with their impatient feelings by becoming angry. Rewards and punishments are clearly used extensively in schools and families to 'control' pupils' behaviour. In a preventative sense, school policies should articulate very clearly how pupils' appropriate behaviour will be noticed, acknowledged and rewarded and how inappropriate, antisocial behaviour will be discouraged. There has been a gradual revolution in school behaviour policies as they try to focus on the former, at least as much as the latter. There are some authors (for example, Alfie Kohn (1999) in his book *Punished by Rewards*) who go even further and state that the current emphasis on consequences, including rewards, actually prevents young people from developing autonomy and responsibility. It is only by developing a genuine internal locus of control that children and young people are able to manage their strong feelings, even when adults are not around to reward them for so doing.

The behaviourist approach also reminds us that social behaviours are learnt in the same way as any other behaviour. This is frequently forgotten by teachers who leap to consider rewards and consequences when a pupil is producing angry, aggressive and uncontrolled behaviour that hurts other people. When a child has a reading difficulty we do not start off by considering rewards and punishments. We appropriately ask: does the child know what to do? Then, does he or she know how to do it? And finally, have they had enough practice at doing it? Only if all of these questions have been answered in the affirmative, do we go on to question the child's motivation; and then we try to make it more worthwhile by the judicious use of incentives and sanctions. When it comes to social and interpersonal behaviour, we frequently forget that we should be asking the same questions in the same order. Instead, we often simply ascribe dubious motivations and rush into rewards and punishments. The social skills model discussed in Chapter 10 is derived originally from a behaviourist approach.

One of the reasons why schools tend to focus on rewards and punishments may be because there has not been a curriculum available to teach new skills and competences as there has been in 'academic' learning. A major advance in recent years has been the belief that prosocial behaviour and the management of emotions can be, and may need to be, taught explicitly, rather than simply 'caught'. This may be a response to changing social circumstances, particularly the place of the family, but it seems to be a fairly universal one, at least in advanced western technological societies. Particularly important has been the work of CASEL in the US (www.casel.org) and similar developments in Australia. In England, the development and promulgation of the SEAL curriculum is of great significance. This is not to say that such developments are based on behaviourist principles, but at least they do reflect a fundamental behaviourist assumption that all learning, both academic and social, are subject to the same general principles.

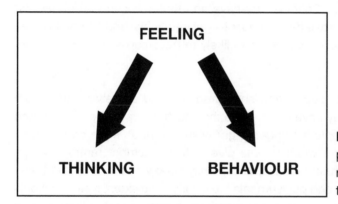

Figure 2.2 Exemplifying a psychodynamic view of the relationships between feeling, thinking and behaviour

Figure 2.2 shows a rather different arrangement of the relationship between feelings, thinking and behaviour. These approaches emphasise the primacy of feelings or emotions that drive our behaviour. Among them are the psychodynamic approaches, first described by Sigmund Freud (Brown, 1967). Central to Freud's understanding of difficult behaviour is the 'defence mechanism', which is designed to protect us from unacceptable, anxiety-provoking impulses reaching consciousness. When they threaten to do so, we experience high levels of anxiety. In order to protect ourselves against this anxiety, we adopt one or more possible strategies or 'mechanisms'. A more popular word for this anxiety is 'stress', which can be considered as a threat to our self-esteem, when our personal basic needs, particularly those of 'belonging', are not being met. Such stress produces very aversive 'negative' emotions, which include anger. One of the defence mechanisms described by Freud is 'displacement', and the application of this to anger is clear to see. The anger vented by a bully on a defenceless and weak classmate may be displaced from anger that 'should' be directed to an abusing parent. But this raises so much anxiety, that the anger becomes displaced onto the victim.

Other important Freudian ideas can be very useful for the teacher, both in understanding their own angry emotions towards children (and staff!) and children's anger itself. They include 'transference' and 'projection'. We carry around with us a vast amount of emotional baggage and 'unfinished business' in which are found attitudes (for example, to authority, to women, or to men), laid down in our unique early emotional history. Freud's notion of transference reminds us of the irrationality of our emotional reactions to people and events.

A development of psychodynamic thinking by John Bowlby (1978) in his attachment theory also emphasised the importance of emotions. At its heart is the notion of a secure emotional base that all children need and from which they begin to explore the interpersonal world around them. This early security and bonding is crucial to the growth of mature interdependence, which begins in childhood and continues through adolescence and into adulthood. When this sense of security is threatened, very disturbing and aversive emotions are experienced, leading sometimes to desperate attempts to re-establish contact with emotional security. Anger is one of the felt responses to a threat to security – as any parent may have experienced when, instead of loving embraces after a prolonged absence, he or she is met with a 'calculated' and punishing coldness. Attachment theory reminds us of the importance of 'belonging', which again links us with a feeling of being valued or loveable, and so with self-esteem. The 'litmus paper' of a school's effectiveness can be described in terms of whether the school really does convey a sense of community, belonging and value to all its pupils. If any children do not achieve this sense of security, expressions of angry, hostile and destructive behaviour are more likely. The existence of 'nurture groups' in a growing number of schools, (Cooper and Tiknaz, 2007; Boxhall and Lucas, 2010) derives from 'attachment theory' and is clearly an important preventative measure in reducing anger in pupils.

Figure 2.3 Exemplifying a more cognitive-behavioural view of the relationships between thinking, feeling and behaviour

The third component to which psychologists give relative emphasis is that of thinking or the cognitive dimension (Figure 2.3). Cognitive psychologists believe that the nature of thinking heavily influences our feelings, and it is these feelings that then drive our behaviour. There are two ways in which thinking or thought processes can do this. The first of these considers how our thinking can become distorted or irrational, leading to negative emotions, including anger.

Psychologists adopting this approach, usually called 'cognitive behavioural psychologists', start with the belief that it is not the event itself that makes us angry, or sad, or depressed etc. The same dreadful event can happen to several people, yet their individual reactions to it can differ remarkably. What accounts for this difference is the way the event is viewed, rather than the event itself. Douglas Bader, who lived for flying, lost both his legs. His reaction was to see this as a personal challenge. A more recent example might be that of Frank Gardner, then BBC security correspondent, who was repeatedly shot in June 2004 and is now a paraplegic (Gardner, 2006). Despite this, he fought back to overcome his loss and devastation and still regularly reports for the BBC on security matters. Another person may well have crumbled, feeling bitter and twisted that life had dealt such a cruel and unfair blow. Cognitive behaviourists maintain that nothing *makes* us angry – in reality, it is we ourselves who make us that way by interpreting what happens to us as an attack upon us, and as being in some way unjustified, unfair. The moment we interpret something as hostile, we become physiologically aroused. This arousal is accompanied by a strong emotional urge to fight back aggressively. In other words, we feel angry.

An everyday example might help to illustrate the process. Wearing brand new leather shoes one day, one of the authors was waiting at a bus stop. Somebody stepped back and stepped on those expensive new shoes, and what is more, scratched the leather uppers. If he had interpreted this as being a deliberate act, he would undoubtedly have become very angry. How he might have expressed this anger may well have depended on whether the person was muscular and six feet six tall, or not! Alternatively, he may have interpreted the misdemeanour as being due to carelessness – he would probably then have been more irritated than angry. How he expressed that irritation, or didn't, may well have been due to the kind of moral inhibitions he had imbibed from his family upbringing. In fact, the person who stepped back was a young mother with two children, one of whom was a young toddler, and it was in controlling the toddler that the accident occurred. Now, we have cause for regret rather than anger, because the damage was not seen as being hostile or due to clumsiness.

One way to control anger, then, is to prevent angry feelings by changing the way we interpret the 'triggers' that normally spark these feelings off. The event is the 'match' in our firework model; the way we interpret the event is the 'fuse'. If we interpret the trigger as an attack, then certainly the fuse will be well and truly lit, whereas if we construe the trigger as an unfortunate accident, and do not irrationally believe that accidents should never happen to us, the fuse will be snuffed out and the explosion prevented.

What is important, then, is the quality of our thinking and our beliefs. It seems that people who experience negative emotions tend to think in certain ways. Aaron Beck (1988) calls such thinking 'distorted', which is a rigid, all-or-nothing, black-and-white kind of thinking. To help angry people control their anger, it is necessary to find out what they are saying to themselves, their internal dialogue, when they are confronted with something that 'makes' them angry. What we find is that their thinking is of the kind described above. Ellis and Dryden (1999) take a slightly different view and focus rather on the beliefs that people hold, finding that angry people have what they call 'irrational beliefs'. Many of the triggers that spark off anger do so because we irrationally believe that our worth and value depends upon what other people think, say and do to us. Name-calling, or racial taunting, for example, has nothing to do with my real worth and value. If I really believed that, it would be very hard to become worked up because of what is said to or about me. One of aggressive children's common irrational beliefs is, 'It isn't fair'. The world has, however, never been fair and never will be. If children believe it, and adults frequently encourage them in such an erroneous view, then it is highly likely that they will become very angry when they perceive that someone has treated them unfairly – and, for that, they should be condemned.

Cognitive behavioural psychologists focus on this distorted thinking and these irrational beliefs. We know that adolescent boys who are more than usually aggressive attribute hostile intentions to what are, in fact, 'neutral' actions. They are hypersensitive to criticism, and likely to flare up and fly off the handle. There are men serving life sentences in prison for murder because someone 'stared' at them.

There is a second way in which our thinking can affect our behaviour. Kenneth Dodge (1986; Crick and Dodge, 2004), an American researcher into aggressive behaviour, sees the problem not so much to do with *what* we think, but in the *way* we think – the processes of thinking. When we enter into any social situation we immediately have tasks to achieve. It may be to face someone who has hurt us, or vice versa, or to join a group at a party, or to handle teasing. Our first task is to 'read' what is going on. We have to take in a lot of information very quickly whenever we enter into any social situation – people's facial expressions, tone of voice, body posture, as well as myriad pieces of information about the context, not forgetting information about our own feelings. The analysis of this information clarifies the task we have to do or the 'problem' that we have to solve. Kenneth Dodge sees us rather like computers who have to process vast amounts of information very quickly and then work out what we want to do and how to do it. Normally, all this process is out of our awareness. Rather like a chess-playing computer, we generate very quickly a series of alternative courses of action, rapidly running through their pros and cons and eventually choosing a course of action that we hope will achieve our aim.

Two aspects of this process can cause us problems. First, we can get into a habit of choosing one particular alternative, and thus it becomes the first one we consider; second, some of us choose that first course of action without considering any of the others. Angry people are typically very impulsive, and there is considerable evidence that young people with emotional difficulties find it very difficult to generate alternative courses of action to deal with interpersonal problems. They tend to get hooked on one, and that one that is not usually a very successful option.

Having chosen a particular alternative, a chess-playing computer then automatically executes a sub-routine. This is the application stage, and things can go wrong here as well. Working with a group of delinquent adolescents, we were trying to teach them alternative ways of handling teachers and the police, who not infrequently had to tick them off. The boys only seemed to have one 'choice' – that of swearing back at the authority figures, which, of course, landed them in even deeper trouble. We were trying to get them to consider the pros and cons of alternatives, including adopting a friendly smile. When they tried this, it proved disastrous! What they thought they were doing and what they were actually doing was very different. When we videoed them practising this, it became clear that their 'smiles' were more like grimaces and sneers – and hence more 'provoking' to adults than even swearing might have been. We had to teach them how to smile socially.

The information-processing approach tries to establish where the problem-solving process is breaking down for the individual angry person. Is it that they cannot accurately read the situation, or that they are unable to generate alternative courses of action, or that they haven't the social skills to carry out the strategy they have chosen? These skills of problem-solving and socialising can be taught directly and can become an important part of anger management training.

So far we have seen how behaviour, thinking and emotion offer different perspectives about anger. There is, however, another very important additional perspective: the biological one. Clearly, there is a genetic contribution to all human attributes and behaviour. Sometimes people misinterpret the work of geneticists by thinking that there are specific genes controlling our emotional behaviour so that some individuals are more prone to anger and aggressive behaviour simply because they have this angry gene. The picture is very much more complicated than that! Perhaps all we say with confidence is that there is a genetic component to the likelihood, or not, of a person experiencing anger. Findings in other areas of research into emotions suggests that this is probably of the order of 40–50 per cent. This means that, everything else being equal, one person might be biologically more than twice as likely to become more angry than another. But all things are never equal, and behavioural geneticists focus much more on what is known as 'gene expression' rather than gene control. Whether or not a genetic proneness to certain behaviour is expressed depends upon many other factors, particularly past (e.g. family history) and present environments. This reminds us of Kurt Lewin's equation: B=f(PE), namely that behaviour (B) is always a function of an interaction between the make-up of an individual person (P) and his or her environment (E) (Lewin, 1936).

More directly relevant from our point of view is the biological significance and purpose of 'emotion'. There has been a growing consensus in recent years that emotions are rooted in our evolutionary history and that they have an extraordinary value in helping us to survive both as a species and as individuals. They have been described as a 'kind of radar or rapid response system' (Cole *et al.*, 2004), which enable us to appraise very quickly the existence of a threat in any situation and then having an in-built action tendency (to fight or to flee) to protect ourselves against the threat. In our early evolutionary history, threats were physical, but later on (as Maslow's hierarchy of needs demonstrates) they are much more likely to be threats to our belonging and self-worth. Because these action tendencies precede conscious thought as they arise immediately and spontaneously, we have to learn how to manage them. 'Emotional regulation' is a new and expanding area of developmental psychology.

This biological dimension relates to the third component of our firework model, namely the explosive material contained in the firework itself. This is the final component of our anger management model. It enables us to learn to prevent the firework exploding despite the fact that it has been lit with a match and we haven't been able to cut the fuse.

New insights and techniques have become available that help us to control our internal emotional impulsivity and so be able to think clearly about how to manage threatening situations that provoke us to anger. It is clear that each of the approaches we have outlined has something of use to offer. To focus exclusively on just one of the thinking, feeling or behavioural components to the complete exclusion of the other two is likely to lead to less-effective ways of helping children and young people learn how to manage their anger. A thorough individual assessment of the history, type and circumstances of anger is necessary to choose the most appropriate way to help.

In the next chapter we will consider what happens to us when we get angry, and explore the long-term effects of problem anger on ourselves and others.

Summary

- There are four components to anger:

  - thinking;
  - feeling;
  - behaviour;
  - physiology.

- The four major perspectives in understanding anger are:

  - behavioural;
  - psychodynamic;
  - cognitive–behavioural;
  - biological.

They differ in the relative importance each one gives to the four components.

Chapter 3

WHAT DOES ANGER DO TO YOU?

Anger is usually a reaction to something, but this does not necessarily mean something real causes my anger. Angry people often react angrily to what are objectively very minor 'hurts', but they think they have been offended or seriously slighted. So although anger is always a reaction to something, that something may be in our thoughts and perceptions.

Anger is an emotional reaction to our perceived needs not being met – and this is potentially a very positive aspect of anger. We need to remember that we call anger (and anxiety and depression) 'negative' emotions not because they are bad but simply because we do not enjoy experiencing them. They are a bit like pain, which is also 'bad' for the same reason – we don't like it. But without pain, we would probably not survive, as it tells us there is something wrong with us physically and we need to change. Anger tells us that we are feeling threatened when our needs are not being met, and this motivates us to do something about it. Anger often drives us either to force someone to meet our needs or to punish them for having failed to meet them. Hopefully, they will at least be less likely to fail us again.

There are three kinds of anger:

- A response to frustration, when our needs are not being met. This could be a need for particular types of food, or enjoyment or status etc. Consider a young child's reaction to being thwarted when denied access to sweets at the checkout, or an adolescent whose parents are insisting that they get home by 11.30 at night. 'Thwarted' is a good word to describe the 'causes' of anger, but sometimes it is also the things people do to us that make us angry just as much as our being stopped from doing something we feel we have a right to do.
- Anger is sometimes used in quite a calculating way to get what we want. This is called instrumental anger, because we use it as a tool or instrument to achieve something. When children see we are getting angry they may be more likely to obey us – though it may work the other way as well, as, for example, when parents try to avoid confrontations by giving way as soon as a tantrum looms. Some children quite quickly learn that the threat of having a tantrum is a very effective way of getting people to back down or to do what they want. Sadly, it is a tactic overused by bullies, whose threat of angry power may frighten us into submission. The anger of the boss is a powerful motivator, which later actually becomes demotivating.
- Anger is sometimes used as a release of pent-up emotions, particularly when we feel rather powerless to effect change and when the situation seems hopeless. Being at

the end of our emotional tether, there is a sense of release when we let our anger out. This is called the cathartic purpose of anger, so that we feel better for having released physical and emotional energy that has been boiling up for some time.

So anger can be a motivator as it can help us achieve our desires or release pent-up frustration. However, 'normal' anger is different from 'problem' anger. Everybody gets angry to some extent at some things some of the time, and that is normal. The essential difference between the two is that 'normal' anger is constructive; it lets me know that there is a problem; it tells me that I need to do something about closing the gap between what is and what should be; and it motivates me to think hard and quickly about what I need to do to close the gap. If what I do works, my anger goes. If it does not work, I need to think again. 'Normal' anger solves problems; 'problem' anger creates more problems.

Problem anger achieves very short-term gains very effectively, but at the cost of expensive long-term disadvantages or losses. The negative consequences are all long-term; the 'positive' consequences are short-term and often illusory.

Potter-Efron (2005) describes what he calls our 'personal anger pie' (see Appendix 13). This pie has eight slices with each slice standing for a 'major area of your life that you have damaged because of your anger'.

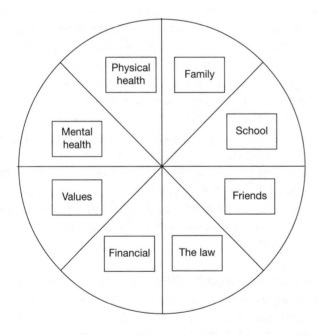

Figure 3.1 The anger pie

Effects on physical health

Anger can be a positive response to feeling threatened – it prepares us to 'fight'. Feeling angry is biologically related to fighting and aggression, just as anxiety is the biological response to another alternative to threat: flight.

Our bodies need to prepare for a sudden expenditure of energy during which significant physiological changes take place. What we all experience when getting very angry includes:

- quicker breathing;
- heart beating faster;
- strange sensations in our stomach;
- beads of sweat or perspiration;
- tense, tight face, and when really angry, often quite pale (though we may go red in the face in early stages);
- tense, taut muscles, especially in the legs and arms;
- pupils often dilated;
- fidgety, small but quick movements.

The process of the body preparing for 'flight' or to 'fight' is kick-started by the brain sending messages to the adrenal glands to release chemicals into the bloodstream. The two most important of these are adrenalin and cortisol. These chemicals are both needed to raise the blood sugar levels and provide energy for the muscles and the brain. Glucose is released to fuel the increased activity of the muscles, but fuel has to be burned to produce energy, and for this, oxygen is required. That is why breathing becomes more rapid and nostrils flare as the body is taking in air, which brings more oxygen into the body. Cortisol plays a major part in regulating the blood pressure and cardiovascular functions in the body. The release of cortisol ensures that the heart pumps faster, the blood pressure increases and the oxygen, transported by the blood, reaches the muscles as quickly as possible. It also plays a part in increasing the clotting factors in the blood in order to optimise survival in situations where the body is under physical attack, i.e. wounds bleed less and heal more quickly. As much oxygen as possible is needed by the muscles, so blood is diverted from where it isn't, at this moment, needed, away from the digestive system (hence the uncomfortable feelings in the stomach and sometimes the feeling of a dry mouth), and away from our problem-solving parts of the brain. To survive at moments of crisis, our biology instinctively forces us to act (to run or to fight), and it does not want us to 'waste time' pondering and thinking. The blood also drains away from the face, which may then appear pale. Sweat and perspiration are the body's attempt to cool us down as we prepare for violent action, which will generate lot of heat as the glucose is being burned up. Finally, the dilated pupils ensure that vision is as clear and acute as possible to detect small sudden movements of our 'opponent'.

This whole process is fine when we really are preparing for strong physical action, as in sport and vigorous leisure pursuits. High levels of physical activity make appropriate use of the changed physical attributes and allow the body to return to equilibrium. That is healthy. The hormone cortisol is often called the 'stress' hormone as, unlike adrenalin, which dissipates reasonably easily as the body returns to normal, cortisol levels remain high for some time. Cortisol levels may remain persistently high in individuals who are often under stress, namely those who may be frequently angry, and this can have adverse effects on the individual's overall health. It is known that high levels of cortisol are associated with a weakening immune system (Watkins, 1997), and with a number of illnesses, including depression and anxiety, diabetes, heart attacks, strokes and reduced efficiency of the auto-immune system, the body's defence mechanism to fight off bacteria and viruses. Too much anger can kill you. As Potter-Efron graphically describes it:

> *The angrier you get and stay, the more likely you are to die young. The red face, the clenched fists. You're like a pressure cooker getting ready to explode. Long term anger can take years off your life.*

Lesser effects of high levels of cortisol include impairment of memory.

Potter-Efron also notes that in other senses, too, anger is a real health risk – we do violent, uncontrolled things in anger, often hurting ourselves in the process. When windows get broken, fists and wrists often get cut. Road rage frequently ends up with serious injury, or worse, as the care and control we usually exercise go out of the window. People get into actual physical fights when they are very angry as well as possibly becoming very angry with themselves, destroying themselves in 'blind' rage. 'Blind rage' is a telling expression as it derives from the fact that we do not see the serious physical harm we are doing to ourselves and others.

Effects on mental ill health

People who are generally pleasant and friendly can become different people when they become angry. The more often and the longer we remain angry, the easier anger seems to become a 'normal' response. In a sense, it is not unlike a drug, in that there may be short-term 'nice' feelings, but with potentially long-term disastrous consequences. Like drugs, tolerance levels change with usage. The angrier we become, the easier it is to become angry – and smaller and smaller slights and frustrations elicit the same or even greater amounts of anger. It can grow and fester to the extent that the world appears hostile and frustrating, so that anger becomes a habit leading to irrational antisocial behaviour which becomes 'a conduct disorder'.

The after-effects of severe angry outbursts or rages are emotionally unpleasant. The release of the brain chemicals adrenalin and noradrenalin in angry outbursts leaves us feeling emotionally flat and empty, often depressed and guilty. In such a state, we are easily irritated and hypersensitive to wrongs and hurts and the whole process can easily start all over again. We may seek health-impacting substances (e.g. alcohol) or activities (e.g. gambling) to dull or distract us from the pain of habitual anger.

Effects on family life

Angry parents often have angry children – and angry children may well produce angry parents. There is plenty of evidence, too, that parents who use angry outbursts and accompanying aggression to control their children play a very significant part in the development of antisocial and delinquent children. Parents who model ways of angrily exerting control over other people are readily imitated by their children, leading to a coercive style of interaction between members of the family, as Gerry Patterson (1986) has convincingly shown. Such families are fraught with tensions, squabbles and fights, with a cycle of bullying and being bullied. Long-term anger destroys effective family life, which is about love and concern, not about fighting and scapegoating.

What about the effects of angry children on family life? Much depends upon how parents cope with their children's anger. We have seen how feelings of anger are related to being thwarted. The reality is that, consciously or unconsciously, parents will never meet all the needs of their children. For some psychologists, the fact of being a child inevitably means that there will be both loving and hating feelings experienced towards parents. How parents handle the expression of such feelings may prove crucial to subsequent adjustment and mental health. Children need to feel that their 'uncontrollable rage' is actually contained – the last thing they need is the parent who buckles in weakness and abrogates control in the presence of childhood anger. There are two extremes to avoid – one, matching the child's anger with your own rage; and the other, allowing the child to feel omnipotent and all-powerful by using anger and threats of anger as a means of control.

Anger, when it becomes a dominant and frequent emotion within families, is pernicious and destructive of all that families stand for. Sadly, angry families are often characterised by the likelihood of serious physical or emotional child abuse, or both.

Effects on friends and friendships

How children get on with others is increasingly recognised as a good predictor of how well they will do at school and at work, and ultimately for the quality of their physical and mental health. Very young nursery-age children who show a lack of emotional control that leads to aggression towards their peers are now known to be at severe risk of forming poor peer relationships at junior and secondary schooling and are at greater risk of delinquency and poor academic attainments generally. Clearly, a lack of anger control and the stability of friendships are mutually incompatible. Friendship is about trust, sharing and concern, and these qualities are poorly developed in people who cannot control their angry feelings. Angry children ruin friendships, and friendships are needed for a satisfying and fulfilling life.

Effects on schooling

School is the place where issues of authority and peer relationships come together in the lives of children. Classrooms should be places where children learn together and where, even more than in the family, issues of 'fairness' are very high on the agenda. Angry people are extremely sensitive to perceived unfairness, and it is 'authority' that thwarts them from getting what they think they have rights to. Angry children pose major problems to classroom management because being very angry is to become 'out of control' – and that is a teacher's nightmare.

One of the reasons why angry children tend to not do well at school is that the teaching relationship is threatened when learners do not attend and do not co-operate. This requires a focus on the teacher and the teacher's agenda. Angry children get caught up only in their own agenda and this threatens the teacher–learner relationship – and therefore they do not learn very effectively. We have seen how intense emotions force us to focus on the 'now' – the future is irrelevant. Success at school involves frequently working for future goals, and we also know that intense emotions shut down the thinking and problem-solving areas of the brain. It is not at all surprising that angry children are likely to be educational underachievers.

Finally, because the classroom is essentially a learning group, angry children disrupt the learning of other children as well as their own. Children learn best in a secure and fairly predictable environment. Angry outbursts lead to behaviours that are predictable only in their unpredictability.

Effects of anger and the law

The relationship with anger and delinquency is clear. Many serious crimes such as physical assault, murder and criminal damage are done in anger. Alcohol and drugs reduce the levels of rational control and encourage angry reactions. Angry children are perhaps more likely than previously to become involved directly in criminal proceedings with the use of antisocial behaviour orders (ASBOs), as is also the case for their parents, with the increasing use of government initiatives (e.g. parenting orders) to hold parents legally responsible for their children's antisocial behaviour. There is also strong evidence that angry children are very likely to become angry adults.

Children who are angrily threatening the security of teachers and classmates through their physical and verbal aggression make up the vast proportion of the large number of pupils being excluded from schools. The consequences of exclusion are severe in both the short and long term. Angry, aggressive students are much more likely to be referred for formal assessment of their special educational needs; for social, emotional and behavioural difficulties (SEBD); or to be moved into alternative provision (pupil referral units, or PRUs). This is the major area in which 'inclusion' policies are currently not working well. In the current climate there is very little likelihood of reduction in the number of places in specialist provision. Without entering into wider issues of special educational provision, there are certainly disadvantages in a child having to attend special provision on the grounds that they pose a threat to other children if they remain in a mainstream school. Such children tend to lose out in terms of the breadth of the curriculum available to them and in the absence of normal role models.

Effects on the general quality of life

Angry people are, almost by definition, unhappy and discontented people whose self-esteem is very low. The way we value ourselves is the measure by which we are able to value others. The more that children believe themselves to be of unique value, because of what they are rather than because of what they do, the less likely they are to feel the need to put other children down in order to defend their own sense of worth. Our ability to manage anger has long-term effects on the values we hold, on the way we construe our part in the community and our ability to sustain meaningful and fulfilling relationships.

Financial effects of anger

Angry people are very expensive! In violent rages, children stamp on computers, throw books, mobile phones and bricks at windows and destroy furniture. Arson of whole schools may be related to issues of anger management. Repairing this damage costs money.

People get damaged as well. The Friday- and Saturday-night overflowing casualty departments and the treatment of injuries inflicted in anger drain the National Health Service of scarce resources. Many of these casualties are youngsters. Special school placements are extremely expensive, and those for angry young people – those with acting out of challenging behaviour – are sometimes the most expensive of all. A figure of £50,000+ per annum for a single child is not uncommon. Surely we should be using these scarce resources more effectively.

Having considered what anger does to us, we will go on to examine what we do with anger and distinguish between effective and problem anger.

Summary

- Anger is part of the 'fight' response to perceived threat.

- There are three major functions of anger:
  - a response to frustration;
  - a way of getting what we want;
  - a release of pent-up emotions.

- 'Problem anger' has major long-term effects on:
  - our physical and mental health;
  - family life and friendship;
  - success in school;
  - involvement with the law;
  - personal, social and financial costs.

Chapter 4

WHAT WE DO WITH ANGER

In this chapter we will look at what we can do with anger, both when we get angry ourselves and when others are angry with us. The way in which we deal with our own anger is likely to be reflected in the way we deal with other people's anger.

Factors affecting what we do with anger

What we do with anger will depend upon the combination of a number of factors:

- learned responses;
- belief systems;
- unconscious motivators;
- individual differences.

Anger as learned responses

The process you consider to be the primary factor will depend on your favoured psychological perspective as discussed in Chapter 2. In this chapter an interactionist approach is assumed, with all of the above factors contributing to a greater or lesser extent to the behaviour we see.

We learn how to express emotions from observing our carers and by learning behaviours that have 'worked for us' in the past. The responses we learned will have enabled us to get our own needs met, albeit only in the short term. Experiences that we encounter when we are babies and young children are internalised and, subsequently, likely to be expressed in our behaviour patterns. Thus, our early experiences of how others deal with anger and how our expressions of anger have been responded to will have a significant effect on how we respond later to our own and others' anger.

Anger and our belief systems

The notion that our own internal thoughts and perceptions affect our responses was introduced in Chapter 2. A cognitive approach to explaining behaviour, rational emotive behaviour therapy (pioneered by Albert Ellis), suggests that it is not the events themselves that make us angry, but how we think about them. Thus, in the firework analogy described in Chapter 1, our own thoughts and beliefs form part of the lighted fuse. A teacher tells a pupil how well he's doing with a piece of work and the pupil 'explodes', tearing his work to shreds and throwing it in the bin. Throughout this book, anger is viewed as a response to a threat that can be to our sense of self, our self-esteem and the way in which we view ourselves, as well as to more tangible things such as getting our own way, our possessions or our personal safety. In the example given above, one possible explanation might be that the pupil is disappointed with his own level of work, wishes he could do better and, therefore, when the teacher expresses pleasure at the work, it threatens the pupil's view of himself as more able than he is demonstrating: 'If the teacher thinks this is good work for me, they must think I am not capable of doing better.' This internal perception results in an angry outburst that appears inappropriate and unjust to the teacher who has been trying to encourage the pupil by giving praise and being positive.

Anger and unconscious motivators

The psychodynamic or Freudian model of psychology outlined in Chapter 2 gives us an alternative way to consider underlying causes of angry outbursts. Within this model, our responses may be motivated by unconscious desires and fears that we are unaware of at the time. It could be argued that motivations bring patterns of thought associated with them and that they (emotions + thought) lead to behaviour.

> *If all I have is a hammer, everything looks like a nail.*
>
> Abraham Maslow (1968)

A person driven by anger may have a preoccupation with blaming others and a desire for retribution. Behavioural strategies to achieve these ends will therefore be chosen. Alternatively, someone motivated by fear may develop behavioural strategies that they perceive as limiting any further self-damage. For example, a child may have been separated from a parent or carer at an early age through death, illness or family breakdown, and may be fearful of forming close relationships for fear of being 'rejected' again. In this instance, the pupil at school may appear to be deliberately picking fights with adults in order to test out the relationship or stop the relationship developing to the point at which the child would be hurt by another loss. These will be unconscious fears, inaccessible to the pupil themselves. Discussing with a pupil why they have been so angry is therefore unlikely to help get to the root cause in this instance and may account for those times when you find yourself thinking that the pupil's behaviour is completely unpredictable, with no obvious triggers. Exploring underlying motivators may be more effective in coming to an understanding of the behaviour, as well as leading to effective ways of helping the pupil to change.

Anger and individual differences

Recent biological research indicates that individuals have predispositions for experiencing emotions to a greater or lesser extent that are rooted in biology (Gardner, 1993; LeDoux, 1994). Emotional reactions are heavily influenced by a part of the brain called the amygdala, and can bypass the thinking, conscious part of the brain located in the neo-cortex. The person who appears to have difficulty identifying their own feelings and putting them into words might therefore show different underlying neurological patterns from the person who appears emotionally sensitive and volatile. As many of our emotional reactions happen out of awareness, those people who are more self-aware will find it easier to control their emotions, as this gives more opportunities for monitoring their responses and considering whether or not they are helpful in the long term. As self-awareness is thought to be the foundation of emotional literacy (Goleman, 1996), a high level of self-awareness is likely to be associated with healthy expression of emotions.

Other individual factors that affect our ability to respond in a controlled, rational way, rather than in an uncontrolled irrational manner, include physical health, stress, relationships, work etc. The way we deal with and respond to these external factors will, however, be dependent upon the internal factors mentioned above.

What we do with our own anger

We may deal with our own anger in one or more of the following ways:

- displacement;
- repression;
- suppression;
- express it ineffectively (problem anger);
- express it effectively (normal anger).

Displaced anger

Anger may be displaced on to a person or object that is not the focus of the anger itself. This is usually because it is considered unsafe to be angry with the real focus of the anger. For example, a pupil who has been in trouble at home in the morning may feel unable to express their anger at home for fear of making things worse, or even risking physical or emotional abuse. It may well be that when the pupil gets to school this anger is displaced on to a tutor or class teacher or another pupil. In the short term, this may leave the pupil feeling better, due to a release of physical and emotional tension that has been simmering for some time. In the long term, however, it is likely to spoil relationships at school, hamper effective learning and damage self-esteem, leaving the pupil feeling guilty and depressed after the event. Neither does it go any way to resolving the conflict that has arisen at home, thereby increasing the probability that the behaviour patterns will continue at home as well as creating a second range of problems at school.

Repressed anger

The term repression comes from psychodynamic theories of psychology as introduced when discussing unconscious motivators. The unconscious part of the mind is assumed to be able to store memories and control behaviour and feelings, without them coming into our conscious awareness. Repressed anger, then, is anger that is affecting our behaviour but of which we are unaware. To understand causes of angry outbursts in this instance, we would have to help the individual bring the unconscious memories and feelings into conscious awareness.

Suppressed anger

Suppressed anger refers to anger of which we are consciously aware, but that is not expressed by choice. We may have learnt at a very young age that to show anger is 'naughty' or 'bad'. In fact, demonstrating negative feelings at all may be considered inappropriate in some families and cultures. Imagine the scenario in which a young child is given a present from the Christmas bran tub at school that she does not like. It is likely that the child will be encouraged to express pleasure and to say 'thank you', irrespective of her true feelings. We are usually encouraged to suppress strong feelings that may hurt others. However, it is likely that we deliver confusing and inconsistent messages when we do not find a way of expressing our feelings accurately. If there is a mismatch between verbal and non-verbal messages, it is the non-verbal messages that will be the more powerful. It is therefore important that we learn appropriate ways to express our feelings, which respect the feelings and points of view of others. Although we would not be expecting a young child to have an angry outburst on receiving an unwanted present, as this would clearly upset others' feelings and devalue the act of giving, it would be important for the child to learn appropriate language and times to express their disappointment in a healthy and positive way.

Suppression of anger may be a way of trying to avoid hurting those we care about, and stems from learning that to express strong negative feelings is unacceptable. This is likely to have been learnt when we are young, so that guilt will be a strong inhibitor for the appropriate expression of anger. Unfortunately, strong feelings that are not expressed may build up until they 'leak' out onto unimportant matters, or 'explode' inappropriately, hurting those we care about more deeply than the original conflict would have done.

There is a widely held view that suppressed and repressed anger may be the cause of depression in some instances. Depression is seen as anger turned inwards on to the individual themselves rather than outward on to the appropriate focus. This can become a deeply entrenched way of behaving, having built up throughout the formative years. Culturally, women seem to be more at risk of guilt when feeling strong negative emotions, as girls are traditionally more likely than boys to have been taught to be compliant and to be the peacemakers in the family. These attitudes heighten the probability of anger being repressed, suppressed or focused inwardly, so that the person feels that it is they who are 'bad' rather than that they are angry at events outside themselves.

Expressing anger ineffectively (problem anger)

Anger expressed ineffectively is likely to be out of rational control and lead to damaged relationships and negative physiological effects. We are all familiar with the feeling that we regret having said or done something in 'the heat of the moment'. Strong emotions can be expressed destructively, lead to confusion and hurt, and get us nowhere in terms of meeting our own or others' needs.

Problem anger is expressed in a hostile, aggressive way and may take the form of a violent outburst involving both verbal and physical aggression. Verbally, we will be condemning the other person totally, labelling them as 'bad' and overstating the case. For example, 'You're completely useless, you never do as I ask'; 'I'll never be able to trust you again';

'You're so naughty, I simply can't stand you any more.' In the short term, this explosive expression of anger may feel subjectively quite good, as it releases tension, gives a feeling of power and sometimes may get you what you want (but at a cost). Long term, however, it is likely to damage relationships and escalate hostility within them.

Our belief systems not only affect what triggers anger but also influence how we become irrational and inaccurate as a result of the escalation of anger and aggression. We are more likely to think that the other person involved had deliberate intentions to threaten us in some way and to overestimate the extent of this. We also become unable to see things from other perspectives and cannot begin to consider the other person's point of view.

Our ability for rational thinking disappears when we lose our temper, and we also suffer the physiological consequences of aggressive behaviour as discussed in Chapter 3 ('What does anger do to you?'). This, combined with the feeling of having lost control, will leave us feeling depressed and low. It will also leave us with an unresolved conflict, for conciliation becomes difficult and unlikely when we are on the receiving end of an aggressive outburst. Behaviours may change initially, through fear of engendering more aggression, but there is unlikely to be any genuine resolution of conflict. Hostility may then take the form of undermining the other person behind their back and getting others on your side (plotting revenge!), and thus escalating the difficulties and making successful communication extremely difficult.

Anger expressed effectively (normal anger)

When anger is expressed effectively, it provides an opportunity for learning and change. The positive resolution of conflict can lead to improvements in relationships and situations that would otherwise remain unsatisfactory to all parties. Anger can be expressed in such a way as to respect other people's feelings and points of view, even when differing from one's own. In this way the expression of anger becomes a positive act.

Expressing anger effectively involves communicating the concerns we have whilst still respecting the other person's right to have alternative views. This quotation from Voltaire sums up the position well: 'I disapprove of what you say, but I will defend to the death your right to say it.' (cited in Dryden, 1996) We need to learn to be able to express strong feelings without attacking the other person as an individual, by dealing with the particular behaviour that is upsetting us. Feelings can be communicated without blaming the other person, and changes in behaviour can be requested positively. The use of I-messages, rather than You-messages (Gordon, 2003) is a core teacher-and-parent skill in relating to children, particularly when they are behaving badly, and is a practical way of achieving this distinction between the person and their behaviour (see Chapter 7). Our own goals can be pursued while still respecting the other person.

A criticism of applied psychology in the educational context is that it can lead to a kind of pathologising of the individual, focusing on negatives and blaming the individual for problems. More recently, the growth of positive psychology has lead to a marked change of emphasis within applied psychology. The person considered to be the 'father' of positive psychology, Martin Seligman, suggests that:

...there are three pillars of positive psychology: First is the study of positive emotion. Second is the study of positive traits, foremost among them the strengths and virtues, but also the 'abilities' such as intelligence and athleticism. Third is the study of the positive institutions, such as democracy, strong families and free inquiry, which support the virtues, which in turn support the positive emotions. The positive emotions of confidence, hope, and trust, for example, serve us best not when life is easy, but when life is difficult. In times of trouble, understanding and shoring up of positive institutions...are of immediate importance.

(Seligman, 2002)

The importance of this positive approach is appreciated at some level by most parents and teachers, but easily forgotten in the heat of anger, whether their own or that of children and young people. Crucially, then, there is a need for parents and teachers to work consciously on the management of their own anger in order to become good role models for children and young people. In turn, they will be better-placed to help children and young people work through their anger, and ultimately this will become a virtuous circle of improvement. Turning this round is a large part of what this book is about.

As regards anger management, the contributions of positive psychology suggest that we move from concentrating only on people with problem anger and refocus on supporting the development of all children and young people, as envisaged in the five positive outcomes of *Every Child Matters* (DfES, 2005).

Summary

- What we do with anger will depend on:

    - learned responses;
    - belief systems;
    - unconscious motivators;
    - individual differences.

- We may deal with our own anger in one of the following ways:

    - displacement;
    - repression;
    - suppression;
    - ineffective expression (problem anger);
    - effective expression (normal anger).

- There are clear benefits to focusing on applying positive psychology, including developing learned optimism and promoting authentic happiness in schools and families.

Action

Consider your own style of anger by completing the following checklist:

When I am angry, I *[tick one box for each response]*:

		Often (a)	Sometimes (b)	Rarely (c)	Never (d)
1.	become cold and overly controlled	☐	☐	☐	☐
2.	shout loudly	☐	☐	☐	☐
3.	cry	☐	☐	☐	☐
4.	completely lose control	☐	☐	☐	☐
5.	use verbal abuse	☐	☐	☐	☐
6.	become physically aggressive	☐	☐	☐	☐
7.	ignore it but find myself angry about something 'safe'	☐	☐	☐	☐
8.	walk away	☐	☐	☐	☐
9.	damage property	☐	☐	☐	☐
10.	hope it will go away	☐	☐	☐	☐

Score your responses by putting a circle round a number, depending on whether you ticked a, b, c or d.

	(a)	(b)	(c)	(d)
1.	1	2	3	4
2.	4	3	2	1
3.	1	2	3	4
4.	4	3	2	1
5.	4	3	2	1
6.	4	3	2	1
7.	1	2	3	4
8.	1	2	3	4
9.	4	3	2	1
10.	1	2	3	4

Add up your score. Scores between 31 and 40 suggest that your own responses to anger may be ineffective as they lack control. Responses between 10 and 19 suggest that your responses may be suppressed or repressed. They do not lack control but may lead to 'leaked feelings' and are unlikely to be helpful in getting your needs met. Responses in the middle range suggest that your style of anger is well-balanced.

Because this scale has not been 'normed' on a large sample the scores should be interpreted cautiously.

PART 2

Planning to avoid the storm

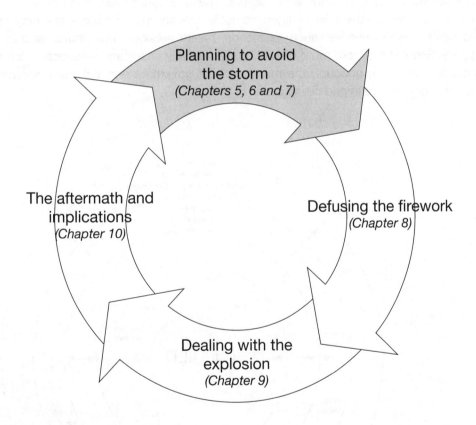

Planning to avoid the storm

Chapter 5

MANAGING SYSTEMS

Storms have a number of defining elements and are a natural feature of the environment and part of a system of global weather patterns. So it is that a brief cloudburst, even of small proportions, is linked to a bigger set of environmental factors. Similarly, a child having a brief but troubling tantrum has an effect on, and is affected by, numerous environmental factors. This is well-described by Bronfenbrenner's ecological model of development (Figure 5.1) as a kind of 'gobstopper', with the child at the centre influenced by a host of surrounding environmental factors. These factors include the immediate or local influences, such as the child's immediate nuclear family and the school, and may also include other close influences, such as friends, health services, the Church and local community. Beyond them are more distant, but potentially important, influences such as the extended family, neighbours, the media, school governors and children's services, including education, health and social care.

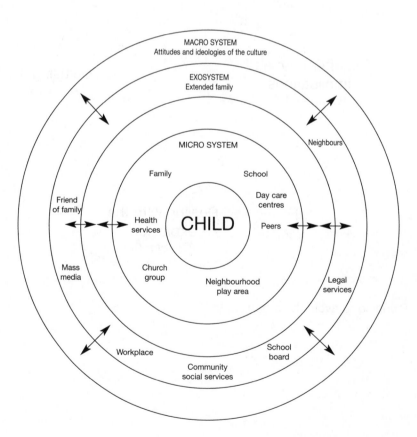

Figure 5.1
Bronfenbrenner's
ecological model
of development

Figure 5.1 shows how complex interrelationships between many factors may influence a child. 'Within-child' factors will also influence how they respond to the environment. Figure 5.2 shows how Bronfenbrenner's (1979) model may be adapted to focus more closely on the factors affecting children within one setting, in this case education.

Figure 5.2 Promoting school effectiveness based on the Bronfenbrenner model. (© Southampton Psychology Service/ISIS)

This chapter will look at only some of the elements referred to above and in Figures 5.1 and 5.2, and is concerned principally with planning to reduce the likelihood that people, adults and children will get angry, i.e. avoid the storms where possible. Children's anger is often less able to be tolerated within institutions, as these are frequently more formal than families and have rules and ethoi managed by a range of people organised within a hierarchy. As the school is the one institution that all children will meet and that is a constant in their lives for at least 11 years, we will use this as an example of how the management of services can produce a profound effect on the outcomes for the individuals within that setting.

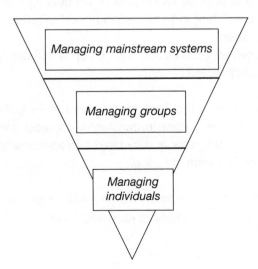

Figure 5.3 Three levels of intervention in anger management

Within a school setting there are three levels at which children's anger management may be considered and these are depicted diagrammatically as in Figure 5.3. This shows that managing anger, in common with managing behaviour, can be tackled at three levels:

- whole-school;
- classroom/group level;
- individual pupil level.

Clearly, for other services, these levels can be replicated but may consist of different detail, e.g.:

- service policies;
- families;
- individual children and young people.

Whole-school factors

A school staff that takes the trouble to work out a set of policies all underpinned by an explicit belief in the maximum possible development of every child will have at least one policy covering positive management of behaviour within a caring and humane framework.

There is a tension between the policy implications of the *Every Child Matters* agenda (DfES, 2005) and the 'Choice and diversity' + standards agenda. This is often seen by schools operating so-called 'zero tolerance' behaviour policies and can result in an over-use of exclusions of children and young people with problem anger, leading to further disaffection and often a downward spiral for the children and families concerned. Thankfully, there are some positive responses to this that can help schools obviate the need for exclusions. These include the programmes on social and emotional aspects of learning (SEAL) in primary schools, and social, emotional and behavioural skills (SEBS) in secondary schools. Also the report of the committee headed by Sir Alan Steer (2005) entitled *Learning Behaviour: The Report of the Practitioners' Group on School Behaviour and Discipline* has been well-received by head teachers and government departments and sets out a number of recommendations including:

- There is no single solution to the problem of poor behaviour, but all schools have the potential to raise standards if they are consistent in implementing good practice in learning, teaching and behaviour management.
- Respect has to be given in order to be received. Parents and carers, pupils and teachers all need to operate in a culture of mutual regard.

There are several references to anger management in the Steer report, all of them in the context of identified good practice, including this one: 'Prior to transferring to secondary school we identified a core group' of "at risk" youngsters and initiated a programme of behaviour/anger management sessions for the first term in school.'

So, there is a growing realisation that whole-school behaviour policies must be positive, be strategic and identify ways to manage challenging behaviour, including anger.

Many teachers and governors complain that policies are simply pieces of paper produced to satisfy OFSTED, and the same teachers argue that the element of 'wheel reinvention' resulting from the development of these policies in every school is a waste of energy. The combined experience of the authors over many years of working in schools suggests the reverse. Primarily, the ownership of a policy is fostered by the involvement of as many staff and other members of the community as possible, and this is further enhanced when the school staff has worked hard to develop a mission with clear aims and objectives, all being pursued within a positive ethos. Schools without such a plan will, invariably, be poor at managing anger and will be characterised by high exclusion rates and poor classroom management skills.

Four main components of a good policy will address the following:

1   whole-school environment;
2   rewards and sanctions;
3   teaching new behaviours;
4   handling crises.

1 Whole-school environment

The whole-school environment, can be thought of as **the ethos** of the school, and includes the physical, curricular, and social environment. This complex set of whole-school environmental factors requires schools to actively consider how to optimise school management style, relationships between teachers, between pupils and teachers, as well as other staff, between school staff and parents, and between staff and other agencies.

Social environment

The existence of good relationships between staff and students promotes 'practices that encourage feelings of emotional security and the development of high self-esteem based on trusting and supportive educational relationships' (Cooper and Cefai, 2009). It is now well documented that the development of a healthy emotional climate can also be supported by peer group involvement within school life.

Jenny Mosely (www.circletime.co.uk) has extended her original circle time model, a widely acknowledged process for improving children's communication, emotional and social skills, to an ecosystemic model she calls Whole School Quality Circle Time. She describes this as 'a democratic and practical school management system which addresses social, emotional and behavioural issues through a systemic approach'. This model incorporates the same systems for the staff as for the children, thus creating an ethos that encourages both adults and children to have a sense of real belonging to the school community and to be able to take risks and flourish without fear of damaging relationships and self-esteem. Clearly, this is going to enhance learning more generally.

Other ways of incorporating peer group involvement include peer tutoring, peer mediation, peer support etc. This has been shown to improve social acceptance, a sense of belonging, academic motivation and empathy. Seeking student views on school policies and development also empowers them to take more control and responsibility and reduces the likelihood of disengagement of the students. These are all identified within Maslow's hierarchy of needs (see Chapter 1) as necessary prerequisites to effective learning and development.

Physical environment

The betterment of the physical environment, even on a tight budget, is likely to have a positive impact on how both children and staff behave. For example, the use of carpets and other soft furnishings significantly reduces noise levels and 'humanises' the school setting, which in turn tends to improve behaviour. We know how differently we feel, and therefore behave, in contrasting physical environments; the sparse village hall and the comfortable hotel lounge, for example. There are a number of resources that can help to analyse the physical environment in the school and play areas, and it is not the brief of this book to go into more detail here.

Curricular environment

There is a growing body of research exploring the perceptions of students who have been excluded from mainstream schools for social, emotional and behavioural reasons. The relevance of the curriculum and the level of support available for curriculum activities are identified as consistent themes. There is a basic tension within our education system between raising educational standards and improving educational access for vulnerable students. However, if we are to make any headway with improving the life chances of vulnerable/at risk children and young people this is an area that must be considered with care.

2 Rewards and sanctions

Second, the policy requires the establishment of a range of **rewards and sanctions** all aimed at encouraging appropriate, and discouraging inappropriate, behaviour. Rewards need to be age-appropriate, predictable, valued and ethically sound, and are best given for a variety of reasons including effort, achievement, appropriate conformity, and courtesy. Similar parameters for sanctions or consequences are needed, but the reasons for giving them need to be fully transparent and well understood by staff, governors, pupils and parents in order to head off unnecessary confrontation.

Some practitioners may think that children and young people should be internally motivated to achieve and behave well and that external motivators are inappropriate. However, children only learn to internalise their motivation over time and in conjunction with feeling that they want to belong to their family's values and belief systems. Some of our more damaged children and young people may not have had this opportunity as they were growing up and may therefore need to learn this in the same way as we accept that other social skills need to be learnt. Good relationships with adults, and wanting to belong and feel valued within the school setting, are vital aspects of helping children to engage, value themselves and move towards valuing their own contributions to school and the wider community.

3 Teaching new behaviours

Third, the policy needs to have an emphasis on **teaching new behaviours**, which may come through a variety of cross-curricular themes as part of:

- personal, social, and health education (PSHE);
- social and emotional aspects of learning (SEAL);
- social and emotional behaviour skills (SEBS);
- National Healthy Schools Programme (NHSP);
- pastoral care programme;
- citizenship and values education.

Having an active programme of social skills training, and running anger management groups should be given serious consideration. This may require support from outside agencies such as the Educational Psychology Service, particularly in the development phase of these practices (Woodcock, in press).

4 Handling crises

Fourth, the policy needs to explicitly address the school's approach to **handling crises**, which will inevitably occur even in a very well run school. Every school now has a duty to have a clear policy for preventing bullying and for responding to it when it happens. There should be robust contingency plans for dealing with fights, bullying, vandalism, verbal abuse and generally disruptive behaviour. The arrangements for dealing with any of these events should be known to staff, governors, pupils and parents, and should be consistent with ethical and professional practices. This area will be dealt with in more detail in Chapter 9.

School behaviour policies

Very few behaviour policies drawn up by schools currently address the issue of anger, and many simply expect children to conform and have no explicit strategies for either reacting effectively or, better still, teaching children how they might better manage their anger at school. The SEAL curriculum provides schools with a well-considered framework for educating pupils about the importance of understanding and managing their emotional lives. The resurgence of nurture groups (Bennathan and Boxhall, 2000), small groups of children/young people who are supported to develop their social, emotional and behaviour skills within the mainstream setting, are also providing promising results, particularly with children whose difficulties are primarily with conduct and social skills.

If each of the four components described above is covered well, the policy is highly likely to lead to the school being both efficient and effective, irrespective of whether it is pupils, parents, staff or OFSTED doing the evaluation. In a fascinating study, *Success Against the Odds: Effective Schools in Disadvantaged Areas*, by the National Commission on Education (1996), there are ten features of success listed, and these are summarised below since they are also highly likely to be features of schools with excellent management of behaviour. At first sight, many of these factors appear only distantly related to anger management, but in practice, a school could use each of these as headings to design part of their anger management strategy:

1   Strong leadership by the head in identifying anger management as a priority component of a behaviour policy.
2   Good atmosphere from shared values and attractive environment – for example, values concerning anger management.
3   High expectations of pupils in terms of effective anger management.
4   Clear focus on teaching and learning of anger management strategies for teachers and pupils to use.
5   Good assessment of pupils.
6   Pupils share responsibility for learning.
7   Pupils participate in the life of the school.
8   Incentives for pupils to succeed.
9   Parental involvement.
10 Extracurricular activities to broaden pupils' interests and build good relationships in school. This is in relation to 'extended schools' (Children Act 2005; *Every Child Matters* (DfES, 2005)) where schools are asked to work with a range of partners to provide extra services to students, and their families and communities. 'Extended schools' guidance has been tested out by some local authorities. Findings to date suggest that there is no single blueprint. There are, however, key or even core menu options. These include:
    – study support;
    – parenting support;
    – sports;
    – art.

Health and social care involvement is found to be crucial to the efficacy of this agenda. It is of note that in some areas (e.g. Southampton), schools have banded together to fund more social care specifically to support families within the community.

The key points for success within extended schools can be summarised as:

•   importance of integration into whole-school policy – not bolt-ons;
•   leadership and management of activities – the school needs to have appropriate capacity and the right mix of skills;
•   clarity about expectations, particularly the links between attainment and non-curricular activities;
•   consideration of organisational structures;
•   understanding of the importance of cultural issues and commitment to multi-agency approaches.

The challenge is to ensure that the approach develops and adds value to services for children and families and to the wider goals of the community, particularly as locality working begins to identify unmet needs within each area.

Summary

Planning to avoid a storm involves looking at the whole environment that the pupil is interacting with. Management must therefore consider:

- understanding the wider system affecting the behaviour of adults, children and young people;

- analysing the relative factors influencing:

  - the child;
  - the teacher/professional/practitioner;
  - the parent/carer;
  - the school/children's service;
  - the local community;
  - society.

- helping a school to construct a policy that is sophisticated, effective and fair, includes preventative approaches, and requires the school to formulate, implement and review policies covering:

  - whole school;
  - classrooms/groups;
  - individuals;
  - working as part of the wider community;
  - effective links with outside agencies, including housing, police and voluntary agencies, as well as the more traditional links with the local authority and health services.

Action

Schools need to consider the following factors when drafting a positive behaviour management policy:

1. Who is contributing to policy formulation?
    staff   *governors*   *parents*   *pupils*   *other agencies*

2. What are/is the school's:
    aims   *values*   *ethos?*

3. Whose behaviour do we mean?
    pupils'   *teachers'*   *parents'*   *other staff's*   *visitors'*

4. Are the school rules:
    implicit?   *explicit?*   *widely known?*

5. How is appropriate behaviour encouraged?
    by parents   *with praise*   *with rewards*   *with celebrations*

6. How is inappropriate behaviour discouraged?
    by parents   *with*   *with*   *by*   *reparation*
                   consequences   *sanctions*   *recording*

7. Are there explicit criteria for the use of sanctions?
    detention   *tasks*   *parents called* *exclusion*

8. How is bullying dealt with?
    policy   *no-blame*   *parental involvement*
                     approach

9. How is self-discipline encouraged?
    relationships *openness*   *trust*   *choice*

10. How is self-esteem promoted?
    language   *rewards*   *programmes*   *monitoring*

11. How are staff supported?
    training   *peers*   *management*   *other agencies*

12. How are policies made fair?
    age   *gender*   *race*   *special needs*

13. How are policies evaluated?
    review   *revision*   *training*   *resources*

Having answered these questions, a school will have identified current strengths and weaknesses in their positive behaviour management policy and can then proceed to develop it more effectively.

Chapter 6

MANAGING OURSELVES

This chapter explores what adults can do before engaging directly with children/pupils. We know that children react differently in a variety of contexts and with different adults. Although some of these factors will be fixed – e.g. personality traits, institutional requirements – there are ways of improving the chances that the children/young people you work with stay calm, engaged and exhibit prosocial behaviour.

Managing classes or groups

In addition to the whole-school factors discussed in the previous chapter, consideration needs to be given specifically to a school-wide class or group management model that promotes an approach to anger management. This will feature:

- consistency – both of practice within and between teachers and other staff, which means that rules, rewards and sanctions all need to be relevant, reasonable and implemented by everyone, using broadly agreed criteria;
- high expectations of behaviour and achievement – which need to be matched by a reward system that has equal access for all, irrespective of ability. Rewards need to be real, appropriate and relatively immediate, and delivered in a way that makes it possible to receive them (for some youngsters this may be non-public and subtle, as they have difficulty coping with praise after years of not getting any). Class-wide reinforcement is also a powerful motivator, and can be used to turn round the behaviour of some very angry children if they are given a real opportunity to support the class in achieving a goal. This also takes advantage of peer support in increasing effective teaching and learning in all areas of the curriculum;
- cohesiveness – so that a prosocial atmosphere is created by staff being fair and holding to agreed values made explicit to children, parents and each other;
- constancy – in as much as the classroom environment should be relatively predictable with changes made gradually in an evolutionary way, wherever possible;
- satisfaction – both for teachers and learners, and most likely to be achieved by differentiation of work to a level that puts success within the grasp of every pupil most, if not all, of the time.

The school-wide class or group management model should also aim to reduce:

- competition – which may be unhealthy if it is based on a need simply to out-perform a less-able peer, and consequently divert energy from the pursuit of individual

excellence within a climate of mutual respect. Competition within a climate of mutual respect and appreciation can be a healthy and effective motivator, however;
- confrontation – between adults and children should generally be avoided in open classroom, and guidelines on how to do this are described in Chapter 8.

Adults' emotional well-being

We have discussed the importance of teaching children the five elements of emotional health and well-being: self-awareness, managing feelings, motivation, empathy, and social skills. It is equally important that we relate these elements to ourselves in order that we optimise our relationships with children, young people and their families, as well as continuing to improve our own emotional and social well-being.

Some of the effects of these five skills are highlighted below as illustrations of good practice within our relationships with children and young people.

Self-awareness

We know that the way we feel and behave is inextricably linked with how others perceive and react to us, but it is more difficult to be aware of the attitudes, feelings and behaviours that are driving us at any one time. We often ask the question, 'Why did you...?'. However, asking ourselves the same question is not easy to answer. It is usually easier to look back at incidents or situations that have not gone as we would have liked them to, and to explore what went wrong after the event. Discussing these with a trusted friend or family member can help us to become more aware of our own contribution to events.

Managing feelings

Looking back at Chapter 4, 'What do we do with our own anger?', can help us to consider how we react when we are angry. However, there are other emotions that can motivate us to behave in particular ways at any one time. Learning to recognise feelings as they arise is an important part of emotional mastery. Noticing the initial warning signs of difficult emotions is tricky, as strong emotions make it difficult for us to engage the thinking part of our brains. For this reason it is considered helpful to recognise physiological reactions that are associated with the emotions in the first instance. Tuning into physiological responses – for example: tense, aching shoulders, tummy discomfort – can give us early-warning signals and enable us to employ strategies that allow us to re-engage our thought processes in order to re-evaluate and problem-solve more effectively.

There are many self-help books on managing feelings, and it is not the intention of this book to look at these in detail from the adults' perspective, but to make the reader aware of the implications that our own strong feelings can have on the behaviour of others.

Motivation

Understanding the way in which our feelings and emotions act as motivators for our own behaviour can be helpful in exploring the drivers for how we react. We have discussed the importance of basic human needs with respect to behaviour. The assumption is that when we choose particular behaviours, we are trying to satisfy these human needs. For example, if it is important that you achieve at a high level in order to feel good about yourself, you may work only towards the outcomes and ignore the effects of what you are doing on your personal well-being. Although this may appear to get you what you need in the short term, it may be at the expense of longer-term emotional health and well-being, contributing to burn-out, for example.

It is also important to understand how early relationships can affect the way in which we respond to current interactions. If, for example, you had overbearing, authoritarian parents, whom you found difficult to deal with as a child, you may find that you overreact when you come across this style of behaviour in children or in other adults. This could be called a personal 'crumple button', as it can be easily pushed by others, albeit unwittingly. It is important to view this situation as an adult and consider how you would now choose to manage it. If you are interested in exploring this further, transactional analysis is helpful in exploring these ideas. *I'm OK, You're OK* (Harris, 2004) has plenty of practical applications.

Empathy

Being able to empathise with other people's emotions is a very important aspect of working with angry children. In the first instance, it enables you to pick up any early emotional warning signs the child is exhibiting. This can be extremely helpful in defusing potentially explosive situations and this is explored in more depth in Chapter 8. Second, getting to know about a child/young person's circumstances can enable you to understand why he/she may be behaving inappropriately. It is important to make a distinction here between explaining and excusing behaviour. Explaining behaviour in terms of unmet needs, as outlined previously, can help to depersonalise behaviours. You are then more likely to feel confident and competent when working with difficult situations. This is not, however, to *excuse* inappropriate behaviour, which should still be subject to the normal sanctions and consequences.

Social skills

It is important to remember that children and young people learn more effectively from how we behave than from what we tell them to do. Most people can be well aware of this when looking at others, e.g. a pupil expressing anger in the same way as their parents, despite being 'told' not to shout, etc. It is more difficult to appreciate the power of being a role model yourself.

If we want the children we work with to behave appropriately, it is important that we look at our own behaviour to ensure that we are giving the right messages. We are trying to encourage prosocial behaviour, which we define as behaviour that enables someone to get their own needs met without violating the needs/rights of others. Conversely, antisocial behaviour is about getting your own needs met, but at the expense of someone else's. An example of this might be for an adult to exclude a pupil from a group in order to win a power battle and make themselves feel better and 'in control' rather than acting in the best interests of the child or children.

It is helpful to look at different ways of interacting socially to help us to decide the most effective way to behave with others. There are typically three styles of interacting with other people:

- hostile;
- non-assertive;
- assertive.

Hostile adults respond to children and others in a rigid, authoritarian manner, often at the expense of the children's feelings and self-esteem. This person is often perceived as unfair, and children behave out of fear and anxiety rather than through making responsible choices.

Non-assertive adults are passive and inconsistent in responding to children's behaviour. They simply react to disruptive behaviour rather than proactively thinking about strategies for preventing it. Children feel frustrated, manipulated and angry, as they do not receive the clear limits they need to function successfully in the situation.

Assertive adults state expectations clearly, confidently and consistently and are prepared to back up words with actions. Children learn to trust and respect an assertive adult because they know clearly the parameters that have been set for acceptable behaviour.

It is important not to forget the power of non-verbal communication. If a spoken message is in conflict with body language and/or tone of voice, it is the non-verbal message that tends to be 'heard'. Consider the different ways that you can say, 'Yes, it's fine for you to go out with your friends tonight' as an example of how powerful the non-verbal messages can be. Try it out with a friend and then watch out for other mismatches between verbal and non-verbal communication. You will find there are more than you had anticipated!

Taking account of the way we think, feel and behave is a crucial element in working with angry children, and preparing in advance will support us in feeling confident and competent when working with them. Confidence and trust in ourselves is often picked up by children, who are more likely to respond more appropriately in return.

Summary

This chapter has looked at how we can prepare ourselves in order to reduce the likelihood of storms happening and fireworks exploding.

We have considered:

- successful classes/groups.

- managing the five elements of our own emotional well-being:
    - self-awareness;
    - managing feelings;
    - motivation;
    - empathy;
    - social skills.

- adults as role models.

Actions for the role model

Consider the following in your position as an adult role model:

AM I?   DO I?   COULD I?   WILL I?

AM I...

- on time?
- positive?
- prepared?
- honest?

  aware of:

  - different learning styles?
  - my own inconsistencies?
  - friendship groups?

DO I...

- check perception and understanding?
- model the behaviour I want to see?
- use encouragement?
- realise I am inconsistent at times?

COULD I...

- change the physical environment?
- negotiate positive rules?
- use more encouraging language?
- listen more effectively?

WILL I...

- make changes?

Chapter 7

MANAGING CHILDREN AND YOUNG PEOPLE

Communication

For young people, it is important they feel they are being listened to and that their opinions are being valued. This encourages feelings of autonomy and being in control, which are particularly important for teenagers. The following suggestions can be helpful in communicating effectively with all children, but particularly those who are demonstrating difficult behaviours.

Assertive communication

- Say what you mean, mean what you say, and, ideally, say it once (but be prepared to repeat it if necessary).
- Use clear unambiguous messages framed positively, e.g. 'I want you to get your book out now' (then praise).
- Catch children being good (instead of simply responding to their bad behaviour).
- Use positive non-verbal communication to back up and reinforce verbal communication, e.g. head shake for 'no' and nodding for 'yes'.
- Use the 'broken record technique' (see Appendix 17), namely repeat your request calmly up to three times (if there is still no compliance be prepared to take preplanned action).

Back your communication with action

- If a child does not comply after repeated requests, issue a warning.
- If non-compliance continues, impose a negative consequence, e.g. staying behind for one minute after class; further non-compliance results in two minutes after class.
- Consequences must never violate the best interests of the child, and should be issued as close to the time of the behaviour as possible.
- Consequences should only be imposed according to a published plan and never arbitrarily or unexpectedly. Here are two commonly used plans showing consequences previously established with the child and found to be helpful:

Teacher's plan	Carer's plan
warning given	warning given
1 minute after class	5 minutes early to bed
2 minutes after class	10 minutes early to bed
send to senior teacher	miss a favourite TV programme
parents called	grounded for a weekend

Other forms of behaviour modification might include the use of a chart with stickers or stars with written targets, preferably agreed with the child. At school, these would typically be about conforming to expected behaviour standards, whilst at home they might be about getting equipment together for school or coming in at an agreed time. Again, praise and positive reinforcement are the keys to success. Reward successive approximations to the desired goals and keep the targets WARM (Workable, Achievable, Realistic, Manageable).

Maintaining self-esteem

Having discussed the importance of our basic human needs, it is important that we take account of this in our everyday communication with children/young people. The use of I-messages helps to convey your disappointment with the current behaviour without directly attacking the other person. Consider the difference between the following two statements:

> *You never bring a pen to class; you always waste half the lesson finding one. How many times do you have to be told to get more organised?!*

> *When people don't bring a pen to the lesson, they cannot do their work and I feel frustrated and worried that you won't get your work done.*

You are giving the same message but explaining the effect it has on you rather than suggesting that the child/young person is completely hopeless because they can never get it right!

Take the blame yourself

If a child is not complying with your requests, it is far more effective to suggest that you have not made your expectations clear than to berate them for not listening properly. This gives children an opportunity to hear the message again as well as maintaining their own sense of self-worth. Children and young people with social and emotional problems often have difficulty concentrating and may need verbal instructions to be given several times before they have heard and understood them. There is also a high correlation between language problems and social and emotional problems – another good reason for keeping communication simple and clear.

Proximity praise

This involves giving an instruction and then finding two people who have carried it out, whilst at the same time repeating the instruction. For example, 'Open you books at page 25 please', followed by, 'Well done, John; I see you have your book open at page 25'; Well done, Amy, I see you have also managed to find it.' This gives children who have not heard the instruction the first time several opportunities to do so. It also enables children who do not follow verbal instructions easily to watch their peers to establish what it is they should be doing.

All of the above are simple, yet effective, forms of communicating with others, which maintain self-esteem and keep the adult feeling calm and in control.

Teaching social skills

A differentiated social skills curriculum needs to be devised by each school, which is endorsed and supported by parents and carers and underpinned by a minimum set of core values. The aim of such a curriculum is to foster the development of all children and young people by teaching them to behave in a prosocial way. The SEAL curriculum is designed primarily as a whole-school initiative, but as with every curriculum area, some children need far more structured and competency-based teaching models.

Specific components of an effective curriculum might include the following:

- ability to introduce yourself and others in a group setting;
- good listening skills;
- appropriate eye contact and good use of other non-verbal skills;
- good turn-taking skills;
- ability to share appropriately;
- good speaking skills (rate, tone, volume);
- ability to follow reasonable directions;
- ability to follow rules of play/games/classroom;
- joining in groups for tasks and fun;
- ignoring provocation and other distractions;
- expressing views, feelings and ideas appropriately;
- seeking help appropriately;
- receiving praise;
- managing anger (own and others);
- forming and maintaining successful relationships with peers and adults.

This list is not exhaustive, and many other skills can be subsumed within the various components. Each of the skills are open to creative teaching methods such as drama, role play, journalism, community service, games, outward-bound activities and sport. Sadly, curriculum pressures and competing demands for time often result in less-creative approaches being used in many schools, with the result that students frequently reject PSHE as unimportant or of low priority. Paradoxically, teachers complain about spending increasing amounts of time in 'managing behaviour' at the same time as spending less time teaching students how to behave.

Conflict resolution

At school, conflict resolution is probably best taught as part of a Personal, Social and Health Education (PSHE) curriculum. If taught to everybody, rather than just children with excessive problem anger, it is likely to be more effective and underpinned by explicit value statements such as:

Respect each person's right to have their own point of view.

Always try to understand how other people feel.

Get your needs met without violating (hurting) the best interests of others.

Deriving a set of value statements that children and young people can own is best undertaken by involving them. Many schools continue to struggle with over-ambitious, imposed values, which are ineffective because they are not 'owned' by the pupils.

At home, conflict resolution is likely to be a far more volatile process than at school, since parents and most carers are not paid professionals with a job description and external appraisal. For parents and teachers alike, trying to teach children appropriate and useful conflict-resolution skills is underpinned by one simple rule (Ury and Fisher, 1991):

Aim for a win/win solution!

Consider this simple 'outcome matrix' for resolving conflict between one adult (parent or teacher) and one child, e.g. getting homework done on time:

Child	Adult
Win	Win
Lose	Win
Win	Lose
Lose	Lose

Accept that 'everybody wins' is an unlikely outcome if the issue is at all contentious, but nevertheless try to give both parties something to feel good about. Acknowledge, too, that this dynamic becomes increasingly complex as the group size increases, e.g. in a class with one teacher and 30 children. However, the following are simple guidelines to promote positive conflict resolution.

- Do not try to resolve conflict if someone is still angry; wait for up to 45 minutes after an outburst.
- Teach alternatives to displaying problem anger (see 'Anger spoilers' below).
- Only use 'I-messages', for example, for a teacher: 'I feel frustrated when people wander around the classroom'; for a pupil: 'I often worry about my homework' (see Appendix 14).

- Try to adopt a 'no-blame' culture by talking about the behaviour rather than the characteristics of the child or young person, e.g. 'shouting upsets me' instead of 'you are always aggressive'.
- Try the 'Step into my shoes' or 'See it through my eyes' routine, where each person has to explain the problem as the other person sees it.
- Acknowledge your part of the problem, however small that is – for example, 'I can see that it could be irritating to be told to do something you don't like doing'.
- Identify solutions or part-solutions as a shared activity, then choose one that is as close to win/win as you can.
- Be generous next time if your win is bigger this time!

Teaching good behaviour

In order to help children learn to read, most schools have curriculum leaders, schemes of work, lesson plans, monitoring, benchmarking, training for teachers, resources and home–school links. However, few schools have had, until recently, an explicit programme for teaching good behaviour and many still do not, which is even more curious since many of them report that concerns about behaviour are at, or near to, the top of their agenda.

Working on the premise that actions speak louder than words, teaching good behaviour is best begun by helping children to do good things, whether they want to or not. Very angry children need help to see themselves as 'good', since they have had considerable experience of feeling the reverse. There are at least two benefits resulting from angry children doing good things: first, they develop a sense of themselves as 'good', thereby boosting self-esteem; and second, their image is improved in the eyes of others (peers, parents, teachers etc.).

Lawrence Shapiro (1994) and others describe how the publishing company Conari Press produced a series of stories called *Random Acts of Kindness*, which ultimately started a national movement in the USA, whereby children in classrooms across the country try to do one kind thing a day (see www.actsofkindness.org for a large number of creative ideas). Empirical research has subsequently shown the effectiveness of deliberate acts of kindness in raising feelings of well-being in the person carrying them out (Lyubomirsky, 2007). Examples of 'kind actions' include: opening a door for someone else; saying something encouraging to someone who is sad; putting some small change into a charity collection. The kindness may be contagious, but even if not, each act is a positive behaviour.

Teachers and parents can help in the teaching of good behaviour by:

- ensuring that children are noticed doing at least one good thing each day;
- encouraging children to keep their own log of good deeds, and perhaps having a cumulative reward;
- giving clear and simple directions on how to behave positively;
- linking to behaviour modification programmes, such as the use of star charts.

Summary

This chapter has looked at how adults can work with children and young people proactively to improve the likelihood that strong emotions will be managed effectively by exploring the following:

- communication – assertive;
- maintaining self-esteem;
- teaching social skills;
- conflict resolution;
- teaching good behaviour.

PART 3

The fireworks

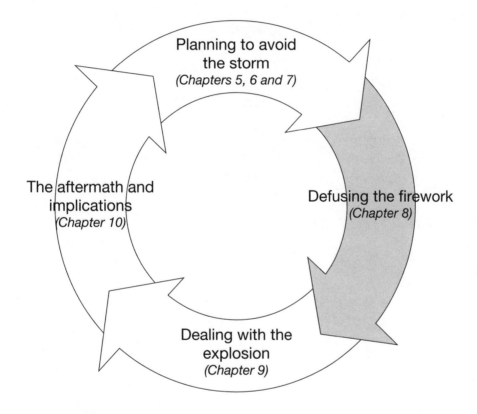

Defusing the firework

However good a school's behaviour policy, schools can never be perfect places. Systems are never perfect, adults bring their own personal emotional baggage, stresses and weaknesses into school and some factors are inevitably outside the control of the school. All the factors we have dealt with in the previous chapter reduce the likelihood of potential flashpoints, but they can never eliminate all of them, particularly to a very insecure and vulnerable child. Added to systemic and adult weaknesses, the behaviours of peers can never be predicted, and peers are a source of many of the matches that spark off the beginnings of anger.

In this Part we will look at how we can intervene effectively during the various stages of the assault cycle. We will explore ways of identifying and responding to early warning signs, the trigger and escalation stages, managing a crisis if the firework explodes, and dealing with the aftermath – clearing up the spent fireworks and considering how to reduce the likelihood of another explosion. The scenarios described in this part relate directly to a school environment but the techniques and underlying strategies are relevant to all adults working with angry children.

Chapter 8

WORKING WITH ANGRY CHILDREN

In this chapter we will look at how adults can minimise the difficulties involved when someone responds to a 'match' or 'trigger' and when the beginnings of an angry outburst could escalate into an aggressive incident. We are discussing problem anger in this chapter, namely anger that is expressed ineffectively and is likely to endanger relationships or safety. It could include either physical attack, which is directed at people or property, or verbal attack, which is personally condemning or abusive. There are two aspects we can consider – what the adult can do to stop the fuse igniting further, and second, the personal skills or competences that the young person needs to learn in order to prevent this happening. As regards the adults, we will consider the most effective time at which to intervene, the importance of early warning signs and some defusing – not diffusing! – strategies.

The part played by the adult

The stages involved in an aggressive incident can help us to understand how and when to intervene effectively and also how our own reactions will affect the direction of the incident.

The assault cycle (as described in Breakwell, 1997) has five stages or phases (see Figure 1.3 on p. 6):

*   the trigger stage;
*   the escalation stage;
*   the crisis stage;
*   the plateau or recovery stage;
*   the post-crisis depression stage.

The trigger stage can be related to the firework model described in Chapter 1, and is an event that 'ignites' a person's fuse, so stimulating thoughts and feelings that lead to problem anger. It is the stage at which a pupil perceives, imagines or remembers an incident or event as threatening. This can include threats to self-esteem and self-image as well as the more tangible threats to personal safety or property. The best time to intervene with young people is at the very early stage, as the body has not yet become fully aroused physiologically, and they are not so fired up as to be incapable of listening or responding to others. Once the body gets prepared for 'fight or flight', and they are reaching the explosion point in the firework analogy, it is very much harder to change the course of events. We are then talking about managing a crisis, which is discussed in Chapter 9.

The escalation stage is the time at which the body is preparing itself physiologically for 'fight or flight'. Adrenalin is released into the body, the muscles tense, breathing becomes rapid and blood pressure rises. There may be some chance of changing behaviour at this stage, but it is becoming increasingly unlikely as the person will be less able to make rational judgements as the arousal increases. This could be likened to the fuse of the firework, and as such will be shorter or longer depending on individual differences. These will be the result of early learning experiences of how others dealt with anger, how our expressions of anger have been responded to, and individual biological predispositions, as discussed in Chapter 4.

The crisis stage is the stage at which the pupil is completely unable to make rational judgements or to demonstrate any empathy with others. This will be the firework explod-ing in our analogy. When under attack it is important that the body protects itself as quickly as possible. This is a basic animal function, 'fight or flight', and as such we share the same mechanisms as lower animals, using parts of our brain that we have in common with our early ancestors. The oldest and smallest part of our brain is similar to that possessed by reptiles. It is pre-verbal and controls autonomic brain, heart and lung functions. It is concerned with the basic needs associated with survival. As it lacks language, responses are instinctive and ritualistic. Reactions when under threat must be automatic and not rely on decision-making processes, which would slow them down. In evolutionary terms, it is far more efficient to respond automatically to a threat than to take time to consider alter-native options with the more highly evolved parts of our brain, which engage language-based, problem-solving thinking i.e. the neo-cortex. Messages from the body to the brain need to take the quickest route possible to optimise survival, and so our earliest survival mechanisms are engaged. Messages at this time do not reach the rational think-ing neo-cortex, and therefore it is very difficult for people to listen to others or understand what is being said to them at this stage.

The explosion or outburst is followed by the plateau/recovery stage, during which the anger begins to subside. It takes time for the body to return to normal. During this stage it is easy to escalate the anger again by intervening inappropriately. The body is still partly prepared for action, and the feelings that accompany this stage are likely to leave the person feeling vulnerable and confused. It is possible that guilty feelings will start to show through, and that these may, in themselves, feel threatening to a young person and esca-late the angry outburst again.

The post-crisis/depression stage is the phase in which the body needs to rest and recover from the high state of arousal that it has been in. The ability to listen and think clearly begins to return at this stage and it is likely that the pupil will begin to feel unhappy about the incident that has just occurred. Guilt often leads to negative feelings about oneself, but it is helpful to make a distinction between guilty feelings about yourself and remorse about the behaviour. Guilt directed at oneself can be perceived as negative as it is likely to reduce self-esteem and make the young person feel bad about themselves. Remorse for the behaviour could lead to effective responses such as apologising, making amends or thinking carefully about how to change the behaviour in the future.

It is important to be aware that the assault cycle can easily be sparked off again if the fuse is re-lit in the recovery phase. We often underestimate how long the last two stages of the assault cycle take and so intervene before the other person has fully recovered. In adults it can take up to 90 minutes after a serious outburst for the body to return to normal levels. If two individuals are involved in an argument, it is possible that they will continue to trigger each other and so repeat the assault cycle for some time. In practice, it is sensible to leave at least 45 minutes, and ideally one hour, before a teacher or parent discusses a major incident with the young person involved. The amount of time needed for the person to unwind will depend on the age of the child and the severity of the incident. Young children are much quicker to recover from strong feelings and are likely to be feeling fine whilst the adult is left feeling drained and uncomfortable.

Early warning signs

Figure 8.1 Early warning signs

There is often an opportunity to stop anger developing into an outburst if you learn to identify the early warning signs of difficult behaviours. This will depend on knowing the pupil well and will take time to learn, but the earlier we can intervene the better.

Intervening in the early stages of an outburst stands a much better chance of averting a crisis than leaving things to develop. This is where identifying early warning signs could be helpful in reducing the likelihood of things escalating. Any techniques that distract or divert the young person's attention from their own distress should be helpful. Alternatively, activities that help the person to relax, and discussion and negotiation, may be effective. Because we, the adults, are likely to feel threatened by the potential outburst that we perceive, we must be aware that our reactions are likely to mirror the assault cycle as well. It is important that we do not escalate the outburst at this stage by getting angry as well. It will help us to stay collected if we are able to distance ourselves from the incident. Even if the anger appears to be directed at us, it is important to be aware that it is also a reflection of the child's internal conflicts and difficulties, and may, in part, result from strategies that the young person has learnt to cope with problems or gain attention. Ways of preparing ourselves to deal with difficult incidents were discussed in more detail in Chapter 6.

Early warning signs can include changes in any of the following:

- physical agitation – pacing up and down, fiddling with equipment, twitching legs;
- facial expression;
- eye contact;
- body posture;
- facial colouring;
- tone of voice;
- verbal challenges;
- position in the classroom;
- rapid mood swings;
- over-sensitivity to suggestions or criticisms.

It is important to stress that these 'signs' will be individual to each child and that knowing the child well is important. We need to take account of cultural differences when focusing on the meaning of specific behaviours, as behaviour has different meaning in different cultures and contexts. For example, the comfort zone (how close people like to be to each other) varies in different cultures, and another example concerns eye gaze – when looking directly at someone is considered impolite in some cultures. Additionally, there are gender-specific cultural differences in what is considered polite or acceptable. Basically, the signs we are looking for will involve a change in behaviour representing a heightened state of arousal. There may be few signs and you may need to look hard to find them. They may also vary according to the environment and the nature of the perceived threat.

At this stage adults often feel in a dilemma, torn between ignoring the signs and hoping the problem will go away, and intervening inappropriately and escalating the behaviours. Ignoring signs of aggressive outbursts is unhelpful, as this is the beginning of an anger reaction that has a momentum of its own once it is in full flight. Some positive action from the adult is necessary. Phrases that are likely to make matters worse at this stage include anything that devalues the other person. Examples include:

- *Pull yourself together*
- *I thought you were more grown up than this*
- *Don't be silly*
- *Now don't start that!*

Although these may seem harmless remarks normally, it must be remembered that, at this stage, the pupil is already beginning to respond angrily to a perceived threat, and the physiology is changing in line with this. People are therefore less rational at this stage and perceptions are skewed to the negative. Finding appropriate ways to intervene that enhance the pupil's self-esteem is one of the best ways to avoid aggressive confrontations.

Defusing techniques that can be used by the adult to minimise the likelihood of the 'explosion'

Figure 8.2 Protecting against the possibility of storm damage

The following strategies may help to defuse the anger and reduce physiological arousal:

1   distraction;
2   relocation;
3   change of activity;
4   physical proximity;
5   use of humour;
6   active listening;
7   active ignoring;
8   reducing physiological arousal.

- **Distraction** is more likely to be effective with younger children. Distracting with a favourite toy or an event happening elsewhere may be enough to divert their attention away from their own distress.
- **Relocation**, by removing the pupil from the environment that is stressful, may avert the escalation of the outburst. For example, pupils can be sent on an errand of responsibility. This has the advantage of supporting self-esteem as well as removing them from the difficult situation. It may be that you would want to go with the pupil if you are concerned for their safety or feel that they may need added strategies to support them. Conversely, if the anger is directed at you, it may be advantageous to allow 'cool off' time without being present. Clearly, it is important that whole-school systems are in place in order that there are agreed procedures for such eventualities.
- **Change of activity** – doing something different – may be sufficient to alter the task that you are asking the child to participate in. It will be important that a positive behaviour programme incorporates strategies to help the pupil learn how to deal with tasks that they find threatening.
- **Humour** is a strategy to be used with caution as the pupil could misinterpret it as belittling their response. Certainly, sarcasm and irony should be avoided. Although it is high-risk, humour can be extremely successful, as the physiological responses involved in humour are the exact opposite of those of anger. Laughter is therefore a very good antidote to anger.
- **Physical proximity** to the child may not be appropriate. Although some children respond well to physical closeness, it is important to know the person well in order to know whether this approach will be successful or not. For some pupils this may add to their feelings of threat and insecurity. This strategy should be avoided when working with pupils you do not know well, though eye contact and minimal physical contact may be helpful.
- **Active listening** promotes communication. For young people it is important to feel that they are being listened to effectively and that their opinions are being valued. This encourages feelings of being in control, which is particularly important for teenagers. It may be that this is not an appropriate time for in-depth discussions about anxieties and feelings, but reassuring a pupil that there will be an opportunity for further discussion at a later time is important. Follow-up work should be several hours after the incident, following which a fresh start can be made.
- **Active ignoring** involves consciously choosing to ignore troubling or challenging behaviour for the sake of expediency and longer-term gain. For example, if a child uses bad language, but under his breath, a teacher may be wise to let it go and focus on getting the child to do something positive. Many confrontations are actually provoked by teachers and carers worrying about every minor behavioural or rule infringement.
- **Reducing physiological arousal** that accompanies the build up of anger, may be appropriate to encourage the pupil to employ direct relaxation techniques, which, hopefully, have already been taught to all children.

    It may be that the pupil needs to release some of the pent-up feelings and reduce physiological arousal by taking part in something physically active, such as running or kicking a football. Other children find music and visualisation (Day, 1994) very relaxing, and there may be ways to allow pupils to either play or listen to music to help them to physiologically calm down.

It is important to remember that when we feel under a perceived threat we are likely to become physiologically aroused and risk entering the assault cycle ourselves. If we do that we are far more likely to feel punitive and to get into a power struggle with the young person that will escalate rather than defuse the situation. We must therefore be able to keep ourselves calm both psychologically and physically. Depersonalising the incident is helpful in remaining psychologically calm. Taking account of the issues that are fuelling the pupil's anger can help us to feel less personally threatened. As a teacher it is helpful to remember that the pupil is angry with the authority role that the teacher has to take, rather than with you as an individual. Equally, ensuring that you have an understanding of the issues that the pupil is dealing with, which are contributing to their anger, can help us to feel less personally threatened. The relaxation, distraction and defusing strategies recommended for the pupil may well be helpful for the adult as well as in avoiding the incident becoming confrontational.

Another issue that causes concern at this stage is whether or not we are reinforcing unacceptable behaviour by providing 'pleasant' alternatives. For example, if a young person shows signs of an aggressive outburst when asked to conform to a school rule, and he or she is offered alternatives when the early warning signs of aggression are spotted, are we encouraging that person to flaunt the rules in future? It is important to separate the issues of avoiding an aggressive outburst and teaching a pupil to choose more appropriate ways to behave. A positive behaviour programme must always be in place to teach the pupil to understand the triggers of the outbursts and to make alternative choices when he or she feels threatened or upset. The consequences of problem anger, however, are so significant that it is important to help the pupil to avoid the outburst at the point at which the fuse has been lit. Understanding and avoiding triggers, which light the fuse, will be an important part of the pupil's positive behaviour programme.

The part played by children: helping angry children to lengthen the fuse

In the first part of this chapter we considered what adults can do to defuse the situation and so prevent an angry outburst. Here, our focus shifts to the things children and young people can do themselves, and our attention is drawn to considering the skills and competencies they need to have and some techniques that they might find useful. Help for children who have problems with anger is at its most effective when directed at helping children to help themselves, so that they can regain the power to have their needs met appropriately. William Glasser (1986) suggests that human beings have five basic needs:

- to survive and reproduce;
- to belong and love;
- to gain power;
- to be free;
- to have fun.

Children who have little or no anger control are trying to meet these needs, but in doing so are less likely to meet them without violating the best interests of others. Our aim as adults is to help them learn the skills and competencies that enable them to meet these needs without harming themselves or other people.

The angry log and the angry thermometer

The first step for people with problems in managing their anger is to understand what makes them angry and how angry they tend to become in certain situations. An activity that helps children of varying ages and ability to begin to develop an understanding of their anger is the use of a behaviour diary or anger log (preferably produced by the child, or with minimum help). This log (see Appendix 4) can then be used to complete an anger thermometer (Appendix 3). The use of these tools allows a child to identify their 'triggers', and then in discussion with a responsible adult, to describe suitable options for managing such people, events, things or places in the future.

The use of the anger log may help a young person to learn to identify and avoid the 'matches or triggers' and so not put themselves in situations where they might become angry. The reality is, of course, that this can only be very general advice and is not really very practical. It is much more often the adults who need to take the initiative of ensuring that there are as few 'matches' lying around as possible.

So we have to assume that in many situations, the 'fuse' will be lit and it is then a question of snuffing out the fuse immediately or at least lengthening the time before it reaches the explosive material and causes the outburst.

In Chapter 2, 'Perspectives on anger', we have outlined some of the relationships between thinking, feeling and behaviour and how cognitive-behavioural approaches emphasise the importance of thinking to the way we feel, and that it is our feelings that influence heavily how we behave. So to lengthen the fuse, it is the 'thinking' that is the most important aspect to change.

Distracting yourself

Some of the ways to change our thinking that people have found useful have actually been around for very long time. We call these the 'anger spoilers' and they work by taking our minds off the trigger by using various ways of distracting us:

- counting slowly to ten or counting backwards from 100, in sevens;
- listing the players in your favourite football team or the hits of your favourite group;
- doing something different that uses a lot of energy, such as punching a pillow or Bobo doll – or taking exercise, like going for a quick walk or run;
- using visualisation:
  - imagining your bedroom and describing it in detail to yourself;
  - imagining a very safe place where you were very content and describing this in as much detail as you can using your five senses – what you saw, what you heard, what you felt, etc.;
  - using the 'turtle technique', imaging yourself to be protected by a shell and simply not responding to any provocation.
- telling someone in charge (who then needs it to be taken seriously);
- using the 'stuck CD' or 'broken record' technique (e.g. keep telling the person provoking you: 'I feel hurt when you call me names but I'm going to ignore it');
- simply walking away;

- being disarming or charming (e.g. 'I'm sorry you feel the need to say hurtful things, because I actually like you/want to like you').

Self-talk and self-calming techniques

Self-talk involves a child recognising the early warning signs before rage develops and then using 'cool-it' thoughts, words and actions. For example, if a child knows that insults directed at her mother have led to massive anger in the past, then use a buzz word to trigger positive thinking, such as 'supercool'. This can then be used to trigger some other thoughts, such as: 'I can hack this . . . I've been here before and I can get past this positively'. If the provocation increases, then repetition is needed and other strategies need to have been taught, too. Self-talk is likely to work best only at the earliest stages of anger, and is not an end in itself.

Changing your physiology

Combining self-talk with breathing and relaxation techniques is likely to be even more effective, so smooth breathing in through the nose and gently out through the mouth can be coupled with, 'I can hack this; I will hack this'.

Self-calming may be further enhanced by actions coupled with self-talk, such as finger counting, using the thumb of the right hand against the fingers, preferably discreetly so as not to draw attention to it. Most important of all, as the evidence is that it markedly affects the way the heart and the brain work together, is to breathe fairly slowly (roughly about six breaths per minute) and as smoothly as you possibly can (Day, 2007). Placing your hand just below your heart near the diaphragm enables you to focus and monitor the smoothness of your breathing. All of these methods rely on changing our physiology; thus snuffing out the fuse by reducing the initial physiological changes that occur when the fuse is lit. This reduces the probability that our bodies will move into the full flight-and-fight response. They have the added advantage of acting as distractors.

Cognitive restructuring

It is a very common misconception to believe that certain things, actions or situations 'make' us angry. In fact, as we saw earlier, in Chapter 2, the same situation may have a variety of possible interpretations and it is the way we appraise or interpret the situation that determines how we will feel and thus how we are likely to behave. If we can interpret the situation differently, we won't feel angry or cross. This very effective way to snuff out the fuse by interpreting things differently is called 'cognitive restructuring'. It is at the heart of STOP–THINK–DO or traffic-light models of anger management, where the STOP is to prevent automatically assuming that the other person has deliberately done something to hurt or threaten us. We feel most angry when we believe that the behaviour is deliberately designed to get at us in some way. The THINK step is to try to look carefully at the motives of the other person and to recognise that things are not necessarily done deliberately but often unthinkingly and accidentally. This skill of not automatically assuming that someone is really out to get us or make us look stupid, and of looking for other possible interpretations, can be explored in calmer moments after an outburst using Appendix 7. The DO is the decision about what behaviours to choose. Having stopped and thought, you are more likely to choose behaviours that reduce escalation rather than increase it. Some practitioners prefer to use STOP, THINK and CHOOSE, as it serves as a reminder that we are in control of our own behaviour and that we have a choice about how we respond. It may also be useful to have a cue card or poster with traffic lights as a reminder to STOP and THINK and DO/CHOOSE when provoked or teased. There are some excellent materials for children and young people using cognitive restructuring methods in Paul Stallard's book, *A Clinical Guide to Think Good – Feel Good* (2005).

Summary

The first part of this chapter considered how and when teachers or carers can effectively intervene by considering:

- the assault cycle;
- early warning signs;
- defusing strategies.

The second part of the chapter described the skills needed by children to lengthen the fuse:

- monitoring incidents of anger;
- self-talk;
- changing physiology;
- cognitive restructuring.

Action

Working with a pupil that you know well, spend some time observing their behaviour in order to identify three early warning signs of an angry outburst.

Early warning signs

1.

2.

3.

In order to intervene at the trigger stage, identify three defusing strategies that you would like to try when you see the early warning signs.

Defusing strategies

1.

2.

3.

Log your attempts and the results.

Chapter 9

THE EXPLOSION

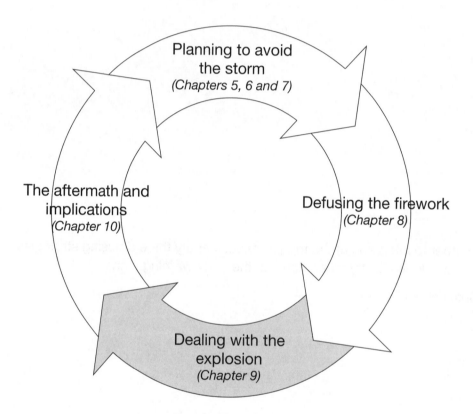

Figure 9.1 Dealing with the explosion

Introduction

In earlier chapters we have discussed the possibility of defusing problem anger at the point at which the early warning signs of an angry outburst are identified. We have also identified ways of trying to avoid the storm, either through environmental means (e.g. systemic approaches) or through defusing individual anger (e.g. by using calming techniques). The importance of teaching children and young people alternative ways of viewing the behaviours of other people, and more effective ways to communicate strong feelings, has also been discussed. There will be times, however, when all the appropriate measures are in place to reduce the probability of an angry outburst, but we still have to respond when children have lost control and are a danger to themselves or others. This is when individuals are in the crisis stage of the assault cycle, and are so physiologically aroused that they are unable to be rational and to see someone else's point of view. At this point we need to know how to minimise the effects of a young person's 'explosion'.

Figure 9.2 The firework explodes

We will begin with practical responses at the point of crisis, go on to discuss how school policy can support these responses, discuss physical intervention as a last resort when all other options have been attempted and there is a real danger to safety, look at the importance of debriefing, and introduce the reader to assessing and managing risk.

Crisis management

In working with pupils who have become very angry, our first task is to attempt to calm them down and reduce their levels of arousal (Davis and Frude, 1995). There is some evidence that calming gestures with the palm of the hand held at about chest height, with fingers pointing upward and making gradually slower and slower up-and-down movements, as though patting the air, can be effective in calming people down. The open palm is a peaceful and non-aggressive gesture and the gradually slowing down of the hand movements mirrors the reduction of arousal that you are trying to achieve. Any body language, tone of voice or body posture that displays power or dominance is likely to be much less effective in calming the person down once the initial crisis or explosive phase has passed. What we are trying to communicate in this first phase is our concern, and that we are listening.

This concern is expressed by demonstrating a level of arousal that is slightly lower than that of the angry young person. This is the strategy of 'mood matching'. If we show total calmness and are completely laid back in the face of an agitated pupil, this is very likely to be interpreted as rejection or non-concern. We should try to express, by our tone of voice, speed of speech and body movements that we really are concerned, but to do this in such a way that we use our own levels of arousal to gradually lower the arousal levels of the other person. Too much 'agitation' on our part is likely to 'hype' up the youngster again; too little, is likely to suggest that you are not really hearing the message. This will be met with a further escalation to make sure that you do!

Angry outbursts happen when pupils feel that they have been threatened or attacked in some way. This attack is often about being made to look small, devalued or being treated unjustly. Angry feelings are frequently due to failure in communication – either because the other person really has treated the pupil very badly or because the pupil has not been able to communicate in any other way apart from exploding into verbal or physical violence. In working with a pupil who has exploded with anger, the task of the adult is to open up communication. This is best done by listening very carefully and showing that you really are listening. This ensures that we give the message that we value the pupil. Together with the calming tactics outlined above, our first task is to give the angry person feedback that we recognise that they are indeed very angry. The active listening skills of reflecting back both the meaning and the sense of what the angry pupil is saying to us is the critical first step. This is all the more important if the child's anger has been a response to something we have done, either by being the 'trigger' (perhaps by demanding some behaviour, or restricting the pupil in some way) or because we have been seen to 'fail' to protect the child against a threat from a third party. 'I can see you are very angry and upset because...' is the message we need to get across, and with it the underlying message that we distinguish between strong feelings that are always 'legitimate', and behaviours that may not be.

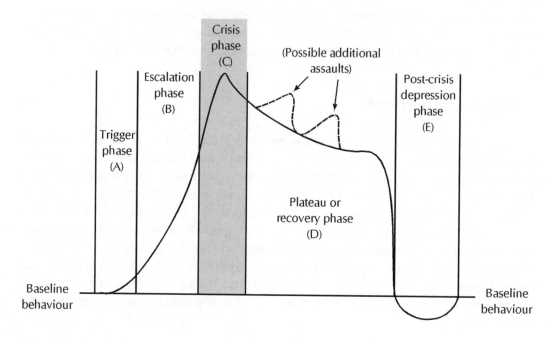

Figure 9.3 The crisis phase

The following guidance relates to adult responses, i.e. at the peak (C) in the assault cycle above:

Do

- remain controlled – keeping completely calm is both unlikely and may be unhelpful, as discussed earlier with reference to mood matching, but maintaining controlled responses is very important; a high degree of rationality and a low degree of emotionality should be aimed for;
- talk firmly and with clear directions, e.g. 'Stop that now', 'Put that down'; you may have to use the broken record technique (see Chapter 7) to reinforce your directions;
- keep talking;
- locate, and move towards, the exits;
- call for help;
- tell the pupil you are calling for help in order to support them and help them regain control;
- remove any audience;
- remove other people if they are in danger;
- remove potential weapons;
- keep a safe distance – violent people tend to need more body space than others;
- assume that the person is going to calm quickly;
- in the case of fights between two pupils, remove the audience and encourage the least aggressive to move away and seek more help if necessary; loud noises, e.g. a whistle, can be effective in distracting pupils out of their aggression temporarily.

Don't

- use confrontational body language – side-to-side is less confrontational than face-to-face;
- engage in prolonged or exaggerated eye contact;
- use confrontational or provocative language, e.g. 'Stop being so childish', 'Act your age';
- use physical intervention unless other non-physical methods of calming have failed, and there are significant risks to personal safety. We have to try to achieve a balance between calming the child down on the one hand and solving the problem on the other. Carrying on with the calming too long means we risk another outburst, because we are seen as doing nothing about the problem (which is usually to do with a perceived injustice or attack); stepping in too soon with solutions to the problem, before the child is calm enough, and we risk another outburst.

Recovery phase (D)

When arousal levels have been reduced to a level such that 'rationality' has a chance (and we need to remember that this probably involves a longer time than we may realise), then we have two further tasks to achieve. The first is to help solve the problem that has caused the perceived threat to the child's self-esteem and the second is re-establish the real world of consequences for unacceptable behaviour.

As regards the first, to engage in problem-solving too late means we can find ourselves with more fireworks! The second aspect that needs to be addressed also requires very careful handling, and it relates once again to the important distinction we have consistently emphasised, namely that between the felt emotion and the behaviour. In a violent outburst, the behaviour, almost by definition, is likely to be destructive and damaging, either to the self or to other people (adults or children) or to property. It is very important that the pupil perceives that there are consequences that will follow from the unacceptable behaviour. The pupil needs to be alerted to this fact in a quiet and unemotional way, and it is probably very good advice to leave it there at this point. The detailed connection between behaviour and the precise consequences needs to be left till much later in the process, preferably several hours after the end of the outburst, even till the following day. It is likely that if the issue is handled sensitively, when normal levels of physiological arousal have returned, the pupil will be able to see the consequences of overstepping clearly defined boundaries as acceptable and just.

Experience suggests that if adults, and particularly those in higher authority, step in too soon, when physiological levels have not returned to normal, and start to lay down the law, often with emotion themselves, and start to administer punishment for unacceptable behaviour, a further eruption is likely to take place, simply compounding the issue. It is better to wait until all emotions have cooled off and then, unemotionally, to put in place consequences that have previously been clearly established. The importance of whole-school policies and clear hierarchies of both rewards and consequences enable this process to avoid many of the side effects of 'punishment', which, when handled badly, simply increase the perceived devaluing of the pupil, rather than the unacceptability of the behaviour. A closed chapter and a fresh start is more likely if the pupil does not feel 'punished'.

Post-crisis depression phase (E)

The post-crisis/depression stage is the time that the pupil may start to feel guilty about the outburst and wish it had not happened. Although the individual is less volatile at this stage he/she is still vulnerable. The pupil needs to feel safe and contained, both physically and emotionally, during this phase and away from any likely ongoing triggers. The long-term strategies for helping to understand his/her responses and how to react differently will need to be taught and practised over time. Strategies to support this process are discussed in the next chapter.

School policy

There should be a policy that specifies a clear action plan for staff who find themselves having to deal with pupils who have lost control. This should incorporate the need for consistency across the school. Staff who are prepared and know what they are going to do in the event of a crisis will feel confident that they have a planned response, rather than being anxious and unsure. Pupils who have emotional difficulties respond well to adults who display a confident air of being in control. Most young people need to feel that they can be controlled by others and find their own lack of control very frightening. The more confident the adult is, the more quickly a young person is likely to calm down.

The policy should include:

- a mechanism for obtaining support from another member of staff;
- guidance on who stays with the class and who stays with the pupil in distress; a fresh member of staff who has not been involved in the conflict may be more likely to calm the pupil, but if the class teacher has a particularly good relationship with that pupil, it may be better for them to do the calming;
- a requirement for individual education plans (as identified by the Code of Practice, see DFE, 1994) for those pupils showing frequent outbursts, to cover the teaching of appropriate ways of dealing with anger, appropriate calming techniques and directions on how to handle violent outbursts;
- information on how to record the incident effectively;
- advice on when and how to involve parents;
- guidance on when and how to involve other agencies;
- guidelines on physical intervention that are in line with local authority policy;
- information on when and how to debrief from the incident – to allow those involved to resolve strong feelings that have been engendered, to allow calming from physiological arousal and to rebuild relationships with the pupil;
- advice about when and how to discuss what can be done to reduce the probability of the incident happening again.

It is important that all staff are involved in developing an appropriate policy for their particular circumstances and that there are opportunities to practise the procedures involved in order to increase confidence. The importance of developing strategies to avoid violent outbursts cannot be over-emphasised.

Physical intervention

The term 'physical intervention' has been used to replace 'physical restraint' as there have been negative connotations attached to the term 'restraint' in the past. Physical intervention should only be used as a last resort and should not be considered unless all other methods of calming have been found to be unhelpful for the pupil.

If it is considered to be a necessary strategy, then clear policy guidelines should be followed and, ideally, staff should be trained and confident in using approved methods.

Physical intervention:

- must only be used in an emergency – where a real danger to personal safety is perceived, either to yourself, the pupil, or other persons', or where there is risk of causing significant damage to property;
- must be in the pupil's best interests – not simply to get the pupil to do what you want him or her to do;
- must be the minimum necessary to prevent harm;
- must not be used as an aversive consequence or punishment;
- must assist the pupil to regain control;
- must not cause the pupil harm;
- must only be used until the pupil has calmed;

- must not be a substitute for positive behaviour management strategies;
- must be recorded in writing;
- must be discussed with parents.

Physical intervention with pupils always carries an element of physical risk and, as such, should not be entered into unless the perceived risks of not intervening are greater. There is governmental non-statutory guidance, *The Use of Force to Control or Restrain Pupils* (DCSF, 2006). The legal implications of this must be considered at a whole-school level.

When any intervention plan is being devised, a risk analysis should be considered to support the rationale for intervening, or not, in particular circumstances. In this way the balance between adult control and individual rights can be considered effectively.

The foregoing relates to pupils who are having difficulty controlling their anger and are losing control when anger is triggered by an event or perceived threat. It does not relate to self-defence issues, where a person is deliberately trying to attack someone. This is not within the scope of this book.

Risk assessment

Risk assessment and management enables a school to plan effectively to minimise risk. It is rarely possible to eliminate risk entirely, but careful planning can enable the school to make judgements about the level of risk and how to minimise it, or mitigate against unwanted outcomes, for all concerned. Risk management involves reducing the *likelihood* of the risks occurring and minimising the *impact* of the risks should they occur.

Five key stages of risk assessment, management and risk identification

1   risk analysis – evaluating each risk's potential consequences;
2   prioritisation – prioritising the key/significant risks;
3   risk management:
     (a) reducing the likelihood of the risk
     (b) minimising the effect of the risk
4   monitoring – monitoring and reviewing the implementation of identified strategies.

Teachers/teaching assistants/parents/carers concerned about 'risky' behaviours within a school setting or on supervised visits outside school should consult their school policy and/or the children's services directorate policy to establish local guidelines for risk assessment. National guidance suggests that all situations that entail a level of risk for pupils/public and/or school staff should be subject to a risk assessment.

Debriefing

This is often overlooked, but it is vital to the development of strategies to stabilise or improve the emotional health of those involved in violent outbursts.

Maintaining emotional health necessitates short-term and long-term strategies for all of us. Short-term strategies should include opportunities to recover from the trauma of violent outbursts. It is likely that the crisis has left all those involved feeling emotionally and physically drained. Opportunities to calm physically should exist with opportunities to discuss the crisis, both for the adult and the pupil. To develop long-term strategies will be necessary to understand the events that led up to the outburst. Think about ways of avoiding similar outbursts in the future, consider whether responses were effective, and depersonalise issues that are outside of our control. Ways of rebuilding relationships with the pupil will need to be considered, and residual feelings, for example anger or guilt, of both the adult and the pupil will need to be resolved. We go on to explore some ways of doing this in the next chapter.

Pupils who have lost control through the use of stimulants or because of psychiatric difficulties have not been discussed in this chapter. This is not to say that the general principles of calming and planning are not appropriate, but that other strategies may need to be employed as well. Particular advice from experts in these fields should be sought in these instances.

Summary

In this chapter we have explored how to intervene at the crisis stage of the assault cycle.

To minimise the effects of a young person's angry outburst, it is necessary to consider the following:

- practical responses – Dos and Don'ts;
- whole-school policy;
- physical intervention;
- risk management;
- debriefing.

Action

- Check your school policy to ensure it includes clear guidelines for managing violent incidents.
- Find out if your local authority has specific guidelines on physical intervention. Familiarise yourself with them, or develop some.
- Practise relaxation techniques to encourage your own emotional and physical health.

Chapter 10

THE AFTERMATH

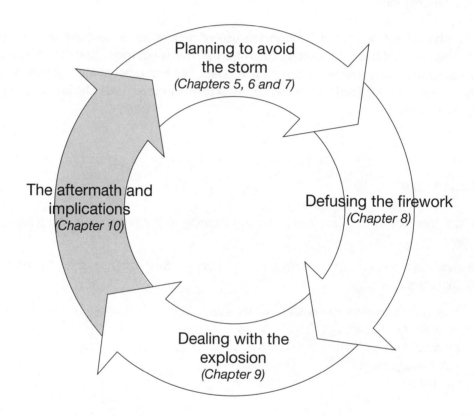

Figure 10.1 The aftermath

We know that the emotion of anger is not, in itself, the problem. Anger is, at root, a biological response to perceived threat and so is essential for our survival. The problem lies in that, unless managed, it leads to aggression and violence. It is the harmful consequences of anger that are the problem, as they inflict harm on other people and sometimes on one's self. Our main focus in this chapter is, first, to look at what needs to be done to repair that harm or damage, and second, how to make such outbursts less likely in the future. As in other chapters in this part, there are two aspects – what the adults need to do and what skills and competencies the child needs to learn.

What the adults need to do

Every school has to have, by law, a behaviour policy. Hopefully, this policy is a vision of the type of community the school wishes to become – what are the appropriate values, attitudes, beliefs and behaviours that build this community; how these will be recognised and acknowledged; and lastly, what are the consequences when antisocial behaviour violates the vision. A pupil-affirming, valuing and non-judgemental institution implies that there are clearly articulated consequences for antisocial, community-destructive behaviour.

This is not the place for a detailed consideration of the place and purpose of sanctions, but one of two points in relation to the damage done by angry outbursts can be made. The first is that there are probably good reasons to talk about 'consequences' rather than 'punishments'. Rather like getting burned when touching a hot stove, it is not the stove that punishes but simply that the behaviour that leads to inevitable consequences. Likewise the community is not seeking vengeance when behaviour violates its norms of respect and safety; sanctions imposed with anger simply model the very behaviour we are trying to avoid.

So in relation to sanctions or consequences, the first point is that, as we have seen in the assault cycle, it is absolutely pointless to point out or threaten consequences when a person is highly aroused – they are in the grip of all-powerful emotions, where the 'now' is totally dominant and where the future (which is the domain of reason) is irrelevant. Any discussion of consequences needs to be done well after the assault cycle has run its course – and we have seen that this is likely to be at least an hour after the outburst, and probably the next day.

The second point is that it is the vision of community and the rules to preserve that vision that need to be emphasised when discussing the nature of the consequences. Tactically, it is often best to ask the person what they think should happen to them as a result of their behaviour. It is a very common experience that individuals in a context of respect and being valued will suggest more severe consequences than 'authority' was considering.

Third, we need to bear in mind that anger is always an emotional response to perceived threat and that this threat is usually to belonging, respect and value. Being judged is often perceived as a profound threat to our self-worth, and therefore every effort needs to be made to reduce the threat. A very non-judgemental approach to destructive behaviour is to reframe it as being essentially motivated to achieve a legitimate need – namely to protect that sense of worth. The question to be asked is therefore never, 'Why did you . . . ?' (which is only asked of us when we have done something thought to be 'bad') but, 'For what purpose did you?' 'What are you really trying to do when you . . . ?' The ultimate answer to that question invariably comes down to trying to meet a legitimate need. The real motive for bad behaviour is, paradoxically, often good. It is the strategies, how we try to protect our sense of worth, which are the problem. There is a fundamentally and psychologically very significant difference between 'You are bad and deserve punishment', and 'What you are really trying to do is to meet a legitimate need, but the way you are doing it is antisocial, hurtful and destructive to our community'. The first approach actually increases the threat and is likely to create conditions of further anger; the second is about teaching different ways of achieving needs. It is about being labelled a 'failure' compared with saying that that you are fallible human being who makes mistakes and can learn from these.

Restorative justice

The 'explosion' that anger frequently leads to almost invariably causes harm to other people. This may be physical hurt, but, perhaps even more frequently, emotional hurt, because of what is said in anger or the damage done to other people's property, etc. Such behaviours violate principles of justice and destroy relationships within the community.

The traditional response to such behaviour is usually a punitive one. This is based upon the widely held assumption that we learn to behave responsibly (and so control our emotional behaviour) by realising that antisocial behaviour will lead to consequences that we do not like. The reasoning within many schools and families is that if the child is punished, he or she will not behave that way again. Although this is to some extent true, there is an increasingly supported view that the real reason why we behave responsibly is much more social in origin: we are really trying to avoid the possibility that people who matter to us will feel justifiably resentful and disappointed with us. The flip side of this is that, of course, if there aren't people who matter to us, we are unlikely to learn to control our behaviour and act responsibly. Punishment actually doesn't help us to learn how to behave in prosocial rather than antisocial ways. It actually seems to make matters worse because it is something imposed on us by people who don't matter to us at all – and this is likely to make us feel even more angry, leaving us even less willing to try to behave responsibly.

What has become known as the 'restorative approach', or restorative justice (Hopkins, 2004) focuses not on the person (the perpetrator or offender) but on the damage done to relationships within the community. Traditionally, when someone has been violent or aggressive, we ask: 'What happened?', then, 'Who is to blame?' and then, 'What punishment should be imposed on the person who has shown aggression?' These questions are fundamentally about assigning blame and dispensing an appropriate punishment. Our motives for doing this are indeed laudable, because we believe that this is the best way to stop the same thing happening again.

You will notice that the traditional approach focuses on events, on blame and punishment. The restorative approach asks different questions. It may start off in the same way – 'What has happened?' – but then switches to relationships and feelings with the question: 'Who has been affected?' And we can only answer that question by listening, particularly to the 'harmed' person, but also to the bystanders and even to the 'harmer'. (Notice how the construct 'victim' is changed to 'harmed' and that of 'perpetrator/offender' to 'harmer'.) The next question is primarily seeking for solutions rather than consequences: 'How can we involve all those who have been affected in finding a way forward?' And the last question is to do with how everyone can do things differently in the future so that the same behaviour does not recur.

Although there may well be externally imposed sanctions in some circumstances, the restorative approach is rigorous in distinguishing between the behaviour and the person who has done the harming – it is the former that is deemed to be unacceptable and never the latter. This is easy to say in theory, but difficult to apply in practice; but what the restorative approach does do is to force us into 'living' that distinction, with its focus on seeking to repair damaged relationships.

In terms of working with a child or young person who has damaged relationships by angry/aggressive behaviour, restorative approaches go all the way from very informal reflections around the questions above to full-blown, formal restorative justice conferences.

Finally, taking our preferred whole-school preventative approach, restorative approaches are only likely to be effective in the context of a whole-school ethos that embraces the values of the primacy of relationships above everything else, with respect for other people and the belief that the best learning is learning from experience.

Peer mediation

We have seen how anger is a response to perceived threat and most of these threats are when we think our needs are not being met. Because we are social beings, there will inevitably be conflicts of interest. The conflicting needs of peers provide a very fertile soil for the growth of quarrels, disputes and fights. As many of these conflicts involve the peer group, it seems appropriate to use the peers themselves to try to resolve conflict in harmonious rather than aggressive ways. So, 'peer mediation' is a process that involves fellow pupils or students acting as mediators (Cremin, 2007; Baginsky, undated). They become a neutral third party that tries to resolve conflicts or disputes between two or more children. Mediators need to understand the principles of conflict resolution and be taught directly the skills and competencies of mediation. Clearly this involves formal training, and the process needs to be closely supervised by a skilled adult.

The skills of a mediator include:

- being a good listener;
- showing you have heard and understood by 'telling back' to the person speaking;
- giving everyone an equal chance to give their story or view;
- staying on the fence ... whatever you think, not taking sides;
- facilitating the identification of the conflicting needs or desires and then helping children in conflict to come up with solutions or ideas on how to move forward.

The stages of mediation sessions are:

1 setting the ground rules:
   - allowing each person to talk and listen without interruption
   - entering the mediation expecting to solve the problem
   - agreeing to be bound by the agreed rules and the solution generated.
2 defining the problem or dispute (with each child);
3 identifying solutions without discussion of their merits;
4 choosing a solution that everyone can live with;
5 seeing if there is a way of avoiding similar conflict in the future;
6 finishing positively – 'Well done everyone for sorting this out'.

Working with individual children

Social skills training

The prerequisite for effective teaching of social skills curriculum differentiated for an individual child in a structured way is a very careful assessment of what skills need to be taught. Children using aggressive, antisocial behaviour are using short-term solutions that do not ultimately increase or maintain their sense of belonging and respect, which is often the very cause of the anger in the first place. So assessment begins with trying to establish what alternative behaviours or strategies need to be learned, and to do this we need to identify what legitimate need the child is trying to meet. Is the angry behaviour a result of a threat to perceived 'unfairness', or perceived disrespect ('dissed') by another pupil, or not winning a game, or being laughed at, or being criticised when mistakes uncorrected by a teacher, etc? Then, having established what the perceived threat is about, the next task is to identify alternative, prosocial behaviours that enable the child to meet these legitimate needs and develop ways of coping when other people violate them. Often these are to do with assertive behaviours replacing aggressive ones. It is our common experience that angry children, very often, have very poor pragmatic language skills.

As with all teaching, social skills teaching involves first identifying the skills to be taught, then demonstrating and modelling them, then giving the student the opportunity to practice them in a safe environment (often using simulation or play, with feedback), before monitoring their use in real-life environments.

Each of the skills are open to creative teaching methods such as drama, role play, journalism, community service, games, outward-bound activities and sport. Sadly, curriculum pressures and competing demands for time often result in less-creative approaches being used in many schools, with the result that students frequently reject PSHE as unimportant or low-priority. However, an investment in the time taken in creatively planning for teaching students' more appropriate ways of interacting with each other and with adults usually pays dividends in reducing the amount of time taken away from classroom teaching in having to 'manage' behaviour.

There are a number of resources that provide more detailed guidance and resources when working with individual children in small groups in these more structured ways (e.g. Spence, 1995).

Solution-focused approaches

When we are helping youngsters to manage their anger, the firework model is undoubtedly very useful as a general framework for reflection and intervention. Focusing on the 'matches', for example, is a very useful strategy for seeing when they occur, how we can avoid them or how we can change the environment so that there are less of them. There is, however, another approach, developed by de Shazer and colleagues (Metcalf, 2003), which also uses the idea of triggers and matches, but in a very different way. Instead of focusing on when and where I get angry, this approach looks at those times when I *don't* get angry. These are the *exceptions*. The focus on exceptions changes the emphasis of the discussion from weaknesses ('When I fail to manage my anger...') to strengths ('When

I haven't got angry . . . '), and from problems to solutions. It directs attention to those situations or contexts when things have gone, or are going, well.

As a teacher or adult working with a youngster with anger management difficulties, exceptions may help us to pinpoint exactly why some situations or people 'press the child's buttons' and others don't. We may need to look closely at when and where (for example, which particular lessons) the youngster never or very rarely explodes; what is it about those personal contexts that is different? If we reflect on and analyse these very carefully, we may well notice that this particular teacher interacts with a pupil in a different way, or that the subject places different demands or challenges on the pupil. We can learn some very concrete ways and ideas that we can use to shift the situation in which a young person becomes frequently angry to one more like those of the exceptions. This comparison can give us a rich picture of the ideal situation we are trying to create for this particular child who is causing themselves and others harm by their angry outbursts.

This idea of exceptions is not only useful for helping the adults to structure the context in ways likely to provide fewer matches for the child; it is also useful to help the young person reflect upon their anger in one-to-one counselling situations. Again, this shifts the focus from possibly accusatory, (at least in the student's perception), focusing on where they have failed, to where they have succeeded. It helps us to ask different kinds of questions such as: 'I notice you didn't lose your temper with John when he teased you this morning. How did you manage to do that?' 'Usually when your work gets handed back to you, and teachers have found mistakes in it, you get really bad tempered, but today you didn't. What was different today than usual?' 'When I asked Mr Jones how you are in class, he tells me that you don't get angry with him or with others in the class. Why do you think you never get cross in his class?'

We have given an example of a slightly different use of a solution-focused technique to work through with the youngster in Appendix 11 using what is known as a scaling technique, and there is a further Appendix 12 for teachers to structure a session around anger.

Motivational interviewing

One of the problems we often meet when working with people who habitually become very angry and aggressive is that they do not see that they have problem, or they feel totally justified in their behaviour. How do we help people to change when the key to change is being motivated to do so? There has been some interesting work done looking at motivation in changing our behaviour. What emerges from the research is that people generally believe that they can get people to change by using the 3F's:

1   FEAR – if you frighten people enough about the consequences of their behaviour, they'll stop doing it.
2   FACTS – if you give people the facts, for example about the harm they are doing to themselves or to other people, they'll change.
3   FORCE – this is not so much physical force as a moral authority, i.e. the person trying to persuade you to change is an expert in the area or has some moral authority over you (for example a teacher, doctor etc.).

Unfortunately, the research evidence in such important areas as substance abuse, teenage pregnancy, health, and lifestyle-related issues, alcoholism etc. suggest that our faith in the effectiveness of the 3F's is grossly exaggerated. By themselves, even all taken together, they don't seem to work very well.

It seems that it is the quality of the relationship between helper and helped that is at the heart of behavioural change. This is explored most fully in work originally with alcoholics, who frequently deny they have a drink problem. It led to the formulation of an approach called 'motivational interviewing', and the principles of this approach can be applied to any situation where we are trying to help somebody change their behaviour.

Early in the 1980s, two psychologists (Prochaska and DiClemente) carried out a detailed consideration of how people change and they found that, typically, we often go through certain stages in this process. It often begins with other people complaining about our behaviour rather than we ourselves thinking the problem is ours. This is known as a stage of *pre-contemplation*. Perhaps slowly, we begin to see that there are disadvantages in behaving as we do and there could be advantages in doing something different. This weighing up the pros and cons of changing is the stage of *contemplation*. At this point, we have an 'informed choice', either to carry on doing exactly what we have been doing, or to change. This is called the stage of *preparation*. If we do decide to change, we then start to put our decision into practice and, often, this involves learning new skills and getting the support of other people, making sure in the case of anger that we avoid the 'matches', that we think about other interpretations (lengthening the fuse) or using relaxation or other arousal-reducing techniques. This is the stage of *active change*, and is often hard work as we have to carry on after the initial enthusiasm begins to wear off. This leads to the *maintenance* stage and, hopefully, our new ways of acting come to be fully integrated with our lifestyle and relationships. But sometimes, we fail, and relapse, and then, to a certain extent, we may have to go through the whole cycle again.

Motivational interviewing emphasises that the key to behavioural change is the relationship and not the techniques. It is a structured and directed approach, but is a totally pupil/child-centred counselling style for bringing about behavioural change by helping people to explore and resolve the mix of thinking and feelings they have about changing. At heart, it tries to guide people to consider certain issues, but recognises that the decision to change is a personal choice and the 'methods' of exploration of the issue are based upon non-judgemental active listening, and valuing of the autonomy of the young person. It is characterised by the belief that change has to come from within and cannot be imposed from outside, and so it is a quiet and gentle approach, never using direct persuasion, aggressive confrontation or argument. Useful publications applying these principles in an educational context are by McNamara (1998, 2009).

Therapeutic stories

These are sometimes called *therapeutic metaphors* and there are a variety of types having different purposes.

First, people who frequently become very angry do so because they feel threatened in some way. To address this issue head on, particularly if perceived (as is often likely in anger) as being authoritarian can sometimes only make matters worse. A useful way round tackling these 'delicate' issues can be the use of stories.

Second, when we are trying to help students 'lengthen the fuse', it is often internal interpretations, attitudes and beliefs that need to change, and these internal processes are very difficult to model and demonstrate. Stories can model these in ways that are impossible externally.

And third, the vulnerability and threat experienced by a child can have its origins deep in the past and operate at an unconscious level. Some therapeutic metaphors are designed to heal using psychodynamic approaches.

Given the different aims of therapeutic stories, it is not surprising that there are different types and different techniques in using them. At one end of the continuum, there are published children's stories that have an explicit purpose in modelling attitudes, beliefs and behaviour. Then there are stories written by an adult specifically for a particular child who is experiencing emotional difficulties, including anger. These are written with the intention of getting across an essential message, by modelling a new kind of solution or resolution with new skills and competencies, and different attitudes, that other people, real or imaginary, have used to cope with the problem situation. Such stories require careful thinking about what you would really like the child to do or think differently about. When given to the child, they do not have to be interpreted in any way and can be given simply as a gift. A very useful resource for these kinds of stories can be found in Brett (1986 and 1992).

A rather different, but well-evaluated, small-group technique of therapeutic story writing has been developed by Trisha Waters (Waters, 2004). These have the advantage of addressing both emotional and academic literacy difficulties at the same time. Groups are run weekly for a maximum of six children. After a short body relaxation, each child writes down a feeling word that they think best describes how they are currently feeling. The teacher suggests a story theme reflecting some of the emotions suggested by the pupils. After some exploration of these issues, there follows some 15 minutes of silent writing during which all the pupils, and a teacher, write their own stories. These stories are then shared in a safe, non-threatening environment. As compared with the first type of therapeutic stories, it is essential that teachers and adults receive training in this method, which has now been used in well over 400 schools in the UK. Further details can be found at http://www.therapeuticstorywriting.com

Finally, there are therapeutic metaphors aimed at helping to resolve unconscious conflicts and traumas. These, essentially, involve projecting a problem on to someone or something else (other people, places or objects) as a way of successfully dealing with strong emotions in a safe and relatively unthreatening way. If a 'dangerous' story is retold in a more solution-focused way, using metaphor, then many children with problem anger can be more open to the indirect messages than simply being told how better to respond or behave.

Richard Gardner (in Shapiro, 1994) has developed the 'mutual storytelling technique' over the last 25 years and suggests that children with conduct disorders (challenging or acting-out behaviour often characterised by considerable problem anger) are deficient in their sense of guilt about their behaviour. Storytelling can enable the child to reframe guilt into a more positive emotion by developing a sense of remorse, whilst at the same time exploring how the child might use this to avoid problem anger in the future. Effectively, this is equivalent to promoting super-ego controls, in psychoanalytic terms, or creating more appropriate self-talk, in cognitive terms.

The mutual storytelling technique involves a child in choosing an object and then telling a story about it. For example, Gardner describes children picking from a bag of toys, which contains animals, people, common objects, monsters, etc. The child then tells a story about the toy and draws a lesson or moral from the story. The therapist can then pick a toy and tell a positive or corrective story, using a similar theme, but having the main character act in a way that involves making good prosocial choices and displaying personal responsibility. This technique can be further enhanced by linking it to behaviour modification, whereby the child, for example, gets points or tokens for choosing a toy and more points for telling a story. Points can be accumulated and used for suitable rewards. If this technique is used over time, the child's work can be built into a personal book or anthology of stories, and these can be illustrated either by the child or using montage, clipart or photographs. A common underlying theme can often be highlighted, which aims to empower the child to deal more effectively with their problem anger in real life.

In practice, such work goes on in schools under the heading of 'creative writing' where it is a feature of either the English or PSHE curricula. However, engaging in this work in a therapeutic context requires training and supervision. Such training for teachers, often called 'educational therapy' has been available for over 25 years, but only from a limited number of institutions in Britain, such as the Tavistock Clinic in London.

Figure 10.2 Quiet reflections

PART 4

Practical applications

Chapter 11

HELP FOR PARENTS AND CARERS

Understanding and managing anger in children

There is anger in every child and in every family – that much is certain. What is not so clear is:

- why some children show much more anger than others;
- at what point levels of anger become worrisome;
- how best to respond to anger when it arises.

Some child psychologists, Melanie Klein, for example (see Segal, 1992), see anger as an inevitable part of normal development. Whether those feelings of hate and anger in the infant and toddler persist depends very much on how certain basic needs of the young child are met.

Our model of anger sees it as primarily a negative emotion, connected biologically to a perceived threat. The response of anger is one of 'fight' rather than 'flight'. If that is true, it becomes clear that there are numerous aspects of infancy, toddlerhood, childhood and adolescence in which the youngster is likely to perceive that they are being 'attacked'. Remember, the important thing is that the person *perceives* themselves as being 'attacked' – it is almost irrelevant whether this corresponds in any way to what is really happening. It is also worth pointing out that a world that does not immediately comply with the child's strongly felt desires can be seen as needing to be fought against desperately, and sometimes viciously. The 'world', that the parents, or brothers and sisters, 'should' not, 'must' not, thwart me from getting the things I see as 'mine'. It simply must not give me anything I don't want either. So there are going to be numerous occasions throughout our early years when issues of 'control' and 'power' are, potentially, occasions for frustration, which may then spill over into anger, either with or without feelings of being persecuted and singled out for attack.

We have seen also that when we feel we are being attacked, psychologically or physically, some of us do not fight, but run away. There are a number of reasons as to why some children respond to perceived threats with anxiety (running away) and others with anger (standing up and fighting back). Which way of acting becomes dominant largely seems to depend upon which strategy is modelled to us by our parents or which one seems to bring us the most immediate feelings of security. Of course, neither anger nor anxiety is likely to be a really effective strategy in the long run, as neither of them help us to feel valued and secure in the longer term. A very general principle – easy to say, but notoriously difficult to work out in day-to-day living, is that the most effective way to prevent the development of angry children and adolescents is to convey to them a sense of worth and unique value. It seems that all our perceived threats really come down to being seen as attacks upon this sense of value. The most effective antidote to anger (or anxiety) is a genuine, passively received message that 'I am valued and loveable'. The more we genuinely feel valued, the less likely it is that we will feel angry, with its accompanying tactics of spite, hurt, put-downs, hate, envy and jealousy.

Differences in anger as children grow up

Children and young people get angry about different things at different stages as they grow up. Some, of course, do not develop emotionally as they should and continue to act in ways that we accept in young childhood, but which are completely unacceptable in adolescence. We expect a two- or three-year-old to be experiencing total rage and frustration and not having strategies to cope with this, so that we may have to physically take control until the tantrum subsides. We consider it very worrying if a 14- or 15-year-old, frustrated in his or her desires for 'freedom', launches into the same intensity of being out of control. We expect the door slam, the sulks and moodiness, the muttering. This may be infuriating, but quite normal.

So one dimension as we move from infancy through childhood into adolescence is the degree of 'self-control' that we can expect. The younger the child, the more raw and uninhibited is the emotion felt and expressed. We do not really know what very young infants 'feel', except through their very obvious behaviour – mothers 'read' how their babies are feeling by what they see in terms of activity level, body tone, type of cry and, most of all, facial expressions. The importance of these non-verbal signals that we give to others about our 'true' feelings remains throughout life, but, of course, we quickly develop the extraordinarily sophisticated tool of language to communicate our inner state to others and to ourselves. As the infant develops into a toddler, the rawness and immediacy of emotional reaction to others and being thwarted begins to give way to signs of self-regulation. By the age of 2, for example, we see attempts to 'control' negative emotions by, for example, wrinkled brows and lip-biting. This is not something that simply happens with the mere passage of time (simple maturation) but something we learn from those around us. We learn to inhibit our emotional expression, to channel these emotions in socially acceptable ways and to develop strategies for dealing with strong emotions. Children as young as 3 can, in some circumstances, deliberately hide their true feelings, and this skill develops as the child grows older. We are increasingly able to put on a brave face or go quiet when upset and angry.

What do children get angry about?

Although there can be innumerable types of things that children become angry about, there do seem to be issues that are characteristic of certain ages. Temper tantrums of two- to three-year-olds and the moodiness and tetchiness of adolescence are examples.

Erik Erikson (1950) thought that we go through eight distinct stages as we grow up and that in each stage we have particular tasks to achieve. If we do not master the task of a particular stage it makes it much harder for us to tackle the next one. Each stage brings with it its own tensions and frustrations, particular issues about which we are very vulnerable and unduly sensitive. It is these issues that – can be perceived as being a threat to us and thus sparking off intense anger.

Stages of childhood

The earliest stage, that of infancy, is where the basic task is that of achieving a basic trust in the world and in people. This is something that we acquire with the sense of 'bonding' with loving and caring mother/father figures. The overall balance of our major needs for food, warmth, affection and care being met is such that we come to see the world as basically trustworthy. The failure to achieve this results in a 'basic mistrust', where we see the world as persecutory and threatening, and thus we become suspicious, quick to perceive attack and hurt. Children who have suffered emotional and physical neglect and abuse carry with them a suspicion and hostility that are very hard to shift.

The second stage, roughly that of the toddler, is characterised by physically standing on one's own two feet, in walking and being able to do a whole variety of new skills. The issue centres around 'autonomy', a sense of being upright and holding one's head up high. Battles over physical control become dominant, often showing themselves in screams and tantrums about toileting. Because toddlers are now able to do many new things, but want to do even more, and do not always have the skills to do them, they become easily frustrated, kicking screaming, crying and generally flailing when they cannot be in control and have their own way. This is the stage of the classic tantrum. The ability of children to pick the worst times and the most embarrassing moments to throw a tantrum is the common experience of many parents. It often leads to us giving in to stop the child continuing with the wobbler, and that leaves us feeling humiliated and guilty. Often tantrums are triggered by tiredness, not feeling well, over-excitement, or when parents themselves are stressed. The lack of adequate language to communicate to you their needs simply adds to the likelihood of the child losing control in a mixture of frustration and anger.

At such times you need to try to re-establish control by modelling calmness and by the use of simple, quiet words to get feelings across. The worst response is to become very angry yourself. In such a state you are unable to provide the experience of boundaries and control the child desperately needs.

The advent of a younger sibling at this age may be experienced as a loss of attention – the subtle and not so subtle pinches and pulls to a new baby are motivated by a jealousy and envy that has strangely angry overtones.

The opposite of achieving an overall sense of autonomy is that of shame and doubt, which can fester away accompanied by a sense of injustice, with the 'chip on the shoulder' variety of anger, with the person unable to rejoice in others' successes, snidely putting other people down at every opportunity. A passive anger, but anger nevertheless.

The immediate preschool and school-entry stage is one of continuing rapid emotional, physical and intellectual growth. Erikson sees the main task to be achieved as one of establishing 'initiative'. Wanting to do everything by themselves, spurning adult help but making a 'pig's ear' of it and then becoming angry and frustrated because they have done so, it often seems as if parents simply cannot win. The temptation to step in and do things for the child can actually thwart that necessary drive for independence and initiative, and can lead to the unadventurous and guilty child who grows into the adolescent and then into adulthood with repressed ambitions and emotions, with the lid tightly kept shut. Such people, seemingly unemotional, can burst into furious rage when the lid begins to loosen. It is often the fear of such destructive rage that, itself, prevents the show of any emotion.

And so we come to school age. Erikson described the task here as one of establishing 'industry', and by that he meant the sense of worth that comes from achieving things by work and effort. The balance of play and work shifts – the skills to be acquired often demand hard work and effort, such as learning to read, to spell, to count. For the first time, too, the family is not all-important – other authority figures, such as teachers, supplement and sometimes contend with the parents in terms of expertise and knowledge. The school child is now being compared with his or her peers, and friendships are part of that feeling of belonging. This now becomes the main task and main source of threat to the child's self-esteem. Because they are sources of threat, they are also triggers for anger. The need to belong, to achieve and to have a standing and status with one's friends become top priorities. These tasks are less easily achieved if the child does not increasingly establish the ability to control and manage their anger. The ins and outs of friendship, susceptibility to teasing, frustration at not being as successful as others, or as successful as one's parents would like – all these provide triggers aplenty for the school-aged child. There are likely to be feelings of insecurity, particularly of jealousy, with the accompanying moan, 'It's not fair'. The 'loss' of the security and support of the family, the feeling of being not liked and left out, and of being bullied and pushed around by other bigger, cleverer and prettier children can lead to a profound sense of loneliness. The failure to achieve the sense of industry is a sense of inferiority. The need to cover up a sense of doubt about one's real worth can lead to a boastfulness and the need to put others down as the way in which anger is expressed.

Finally, as far as we are concerned here, is the stage of adolescence. There is considerable evidence that this is not necessarily the age of storm and stress that, perhaps, the myth of adolescence would lead us to believe. It, like any other stage, has its particular tasks, and hence its particular vulnerability. Probably because they have greater strength, quicker thinking and sophisticated control of language, adults are more frightened of what adolescents can really do to themselves and others. In one sense, adolescence is a bit of a recapitulation or return to some of the earlier tasks – the partial leaving of the family at the beginning of schooling, for example, in late adolescence becomes a reality, with all the threats to security that that entails. Erikson saw the major task of adolescence as being to establish a true sense of one's own identity, to grow away from being primarily somebody's son or daughter, to being somebody in their own right, with skills, values and beliefs that are theirs and nobody else's. Not surprisingly, much of the conflict, stress and perceived attacks are to do with control – about who makes the decisions, about what and when. The importance of the peer group, of peer pressure and 'unsuitable friends', and outlandish clothes and behaviour, all potentially become issues about which adolescents and parents can become very angry. At the same time, puberty brings its own fears and worries. Not infrequently, feelings of anger at their own inadequacy can be displaced on to parents, turning struggles over objectively minor issues into major outbursts.

Status and acceptance become even more important in adolescence, and slights from other young people are taken very seriously, with feuds between peers provoking physical and psychological bullying. The propensity for some individuals to be scapegoats and hounded mercilessly can again be a cover-up for feelings of low self-esteem and anxiety about one's own status.

And finally…

We have considered what anger is, what it does and how we may be more effective in managing it. We have described strategies for preventing and reducing problem anger, and for managing our own and other people's anger. We recognise that this is a task that is never complete. We wish you success in all your efforts to help yourself and others to manage anger more effectively.

Guidance and tips for parents living with angry children are given in Appendices 15, 16 and 17, which can be photocopied.

PART 5

Appendices

Appendix 1

OBSERVATION CHECKLIST: PRIMARY (5–11)

Name_____ Date of birth _____ School _____

Please circle the number that *your* observations suggest is most appropriate and add any *comments* that you think are important.

		Always	*Usually*	*Sometimes*	*Never*	*Comment*
1	Comes to school/class happily	1	2	3	4	
2	Settles in class without fuss	1	2	3	4	
3	Settles in small groups easily	1	2	3	4	
4	Follows class routines	1	2	3	4	
5	Accepts teacher's directions	1	2	3	4	
6	Accepts other pupils taking the lead	1	2	3	4	
7	Appears popular with other children	1	2	3	4	
8	Has at least one good friend	1	2	3	4	
9	Plays appropriately with other children	1	2	3	4	
10	Copes well with disappointment	1	2	3	4	
11	Appears confident	1	2	3	4	
12	Feels good about him/herself	1	2	3	4	
13	Concentrates well	1	2	3	4	
14	Controls anger when provoked	1	2	3	4	
15	Has insight into own behaviour	1	2	3	4	
16	Learns from mistakes	1	2	3	4	
17	Keeps hands, feet, objects to him/herself	1	2	3	4	
18	Hurts self	4	3	2	1	
19	Distracts other children	4	3	2	1	
20	Hurts other children	4	3	2	1	
	Total	___	___	___	___	

Best score = 20   Worst score = 80

Completed by _____   Date _____

Appendix 2

OBSERVATION CHECKLIST: SECONDARY (11–16)

Name_____ Date of birth _____ School _____

Please circle the number which *your* observations suggest is most appropriate and add any *comments* that you think are important.

		Always	Usually	Sometimes	Never	Comment
1	Comes to school/class without difficulty	1	2	3	4	
2	Settles in class easily	1	2	3	4	
3	Settles in small groups easily	1	2	3	4	
4	Follows class routines	1	2	3	4	
5	Accepts teacher's directions	1	2	3	4	
6	Accepts other students taking the lead	1	2	3	4	
7	Appears popular with other students	1	2	3	4	
8	Has at least one good friend	1	2	3	4	
9	Relates well to other students	1	2	3	4	
10	Copes well with disappointment	1	2	3	4	
11	Appears confident	1	2	3	4	
12	Feels good about him/herself	1	2	3	4	
13	Concentrates well	1	2	3	4	
14	Controls anger when provoked	1	2	3	4	
15	Has insight into own behaviour	1	2	3	4	
16	Learns from mistakes	1	2	3	4	
17	Keeps hands, feet, objects to him/herself	1	2	3	4	
18	Hurts self	4	3	2	1	
19	Distracts other students	4	3	2	1	
20	Hurts other students	4	3	2	1	
	Total	___	___	___	___	

Best score = 20   Worst score = 80

Completed by _____   Date _____

ANGER THERMOMETER

Identify your anger triggers by keeping a diary or log for a week or so.

WHAT MAKES ME ANGRY:

Exploding

Boiling

Warm

Calm/ relaxed (98.4°)

Cool

_____

_____

_____

_____

_____

_____

_____

_____

_____

_____

_____

Appendix 4

ANGER LOG

This may be completed by (a) child (b) teacher (c) parent/carer.

Name _____ **School** _____

*Circle the number that best describes
anger management*

Anger at school	Poor		Good		Excellent
Monday	1	2	3	4	5
Tuesday	1	2	3	4	5
Wednesday	1	2	3	4	5
Thursday	1	2	3	4	5
Friday	1	2	3	4	5

Anger at home					
Monday	1	2	3	4	5
Tuesday	1	2	3	4	5
Wednesday	1	2	3	4	5
Thursday	1	2	3	4	5
Friday	1	2	3	4	5
Saturday	1	2	3	4	5
Sunday	1	2	3	4	5

Anger elsewhere (trips, etc.)					
Monday	1	2	3	4	5
Tuesday	1	2	3	4	5
Wednesday	1	2	3	4	5
Thursday	1	2	3	4	5
Friday	1	2	3	4	5
Saturday	1	2	3	4	5
Sunday	1	2	3	4	5

Completed by: _____ (Child/Teacher/Parent)

Appendix 5

ANGER TRIGGERS

When we were discussing the firework model, we likened the match to the **trigger** of anger for an individual. The assault cycle also begins with the **trigger** stage. In order to manage our anger better, we must first identify the triggers that spark us off into an angry reaction. Triggers will be events that are perceived as threats to:

- person or property;
- self-identity or self-esteem;
- getting our perceived needs met.

Once we have identified the triggers that make us angry, we have three possibilities:

- **avoid** the triggers;
- **change** the way we **think** about the triggers;
- reduce the level of arousal by using **calming** techniques.

The following worksheets provide ways of addressing these issues:

1   What makes me angry? (Appendix 6)
2   What do I think? (Appendix 7)
3   How do I feel? (Appendix 8)
4   Keeping calm (Appendix 9).

The following worksheets can be used with young people to help them identify their own triggers, consider alternative ways of thinking about them and identify ways of keeping themselves calm. These can be used in conjunction with the anger thermometer (Appendix 3) and the anger log (Appendix 4) as appropriate.

Appendix 6

WHAT MAKES ME ANGRY?

Stop the match being lit!

Here is a list of statements describing what makes some people angry. Tick the ones that are true for you and add some of your own that have not been listed.

- When people talk about me behind my back ....
- When I get my work wrong ....
- When other people get hurt ....
- When others won't play with me ....
- When I'm treated unfairly ....
- When I'm shouted at ....
- When people interfere with my games ....
- When people stop me doing what I want ....
- When others get more attention than me ....
- When people call me names ....
- When I'm losing at football ....
- When people are rude about my family ....
- When people bully my friends ....
- When someone calls me a liar ....
- When someone pushes me ....
- When I get told off and others don't ....
- When things get broken ....
- When someone takes my things ....
- When there is a lot of noise and I'm trying to concentrate ....
- When I have to do something I don't want to ....
- When I'm told off in front of my friends ....
- When I get interrupted ....
- When people don't give me a chance ....
- When other people are angry ....
- When people don't listen to me ....
- When people don't understand me ....

Other things that make me angry are:

1 ....

2 ....

3 ....

4 ....

Appendix 7

WHAT DO I THINK?

In order to manage our anger we may try to avoid the trigger that sparks us off (as identified in Appendix 5), but as this is not always possible, it is important to have alternative strategies for how we react to the trigger. This involves changing the way we think about the trigger. This gives us more time (a longer fuse) to consider how we will choose to behave.

In the next worksheet, a number of incidents are described. Imagine that these events have happened to you. Write down in the first column what you might be thinking that would lead you to being angry. Then think of some alternative ways in which you might explain the incident that would not lead you to feel angry. It may be helpful to discuss this with a friend or adult. Write this in the second column.

The first two have been completed for you.

WORKSHEET

What do I think?

Lengthening the fuse!

Trigger **Feelings**	*What I think?* **Angry feelings**	*What I think* ***No angry feelings***
Someone pushes you in the playground.	(a) He wants to pick a fight. (b) She wants to hurt me.	(a) He lost his balance. (b) Someone bullied her into it.
Your teacher doesn't listen when you are telling them why you are late.	(a) They don't care about me. (b) They don't believe me.	(a) She is busy trying to sort out another problem. (b) I have picked a bad time. (c) I'm not making myself clear.
Your best friend does not talk to you.		
Someone takes your best ruler off your desk.		
You get told off for forgetting your homework.		
Someone shouts at you.		
A friend calls you a liar.		
You are not picked for the school football team.		
A group of children call you names as you walk past them.		

Think about some incidents that have made you angry recently and see if you can change what you think about them.

Appendix 8

HOW DO I FEEL?

Think about how you feel when you first start to get angry. Tick any of the following statements that apply to you.

I feel hot. ....

My hands start to sweat. ....

I find it difficult to stay still; I get fidgety. ....

My mouth gets dry. ....

My hands go into fists. ....

My body feels tense. ....

My heart races. ....

I breathe more quickly. ....

I feel panicky. ....

Describe three other things that you have noticed about yourself when you are beginning to get angry:

1 ....

2 ....

3 ....

Appendix 9

KEEPING CALM

When we are teaching young people how to manage their anger more effectively, we know there will be times when we cannot avoid the triggers and we are still learning to change what we think. As young people become more aware of their feelings, thoughts and behaviours, they will become more adept at recognising the signs of anger bubbling up. At this stage it will be important for them to identify ways of reducing their levels of arousal in order to reduce the probability of an angry outburst.

To return to the firework analogy, Appendix 6 helped us to reduce the likelihood that the match would be lit and Appendix 7 helped us to lengthen the fuse by allowing more time to consider alternative ways of reacting to triggers. We now consider ways to encourage young people to identify their own strong feelings and help them to choose strategies to help reduce their levels of arousal. This could be likened to cutting the fuse and so reducing the risk of the explosion.

In the previous Appendix (8), the pupil identified some of their own physiological feelings when they are beginning to feel angry, to help them become more aware of when things are beginning to get out of control for them.

On the following worksheet ('keeping calm'), they will then be encouraged to identify what strategies help them to feel better/calm down at those times.

WORKSHEET

Keeping calm

Dampening the fuse!

Here is a list of things that some people do in order to help them to calm down when they recognise the feelings that go along with being angry.

Choose three that you think might work for you and add any of your own that you have thought of or tried.

1   Walking away from the incident.

2   Counting to 10.

3   Talking yourself into feeling calm.

4   Using a catchphrase.

5   Pretending to be somewhere else.

6   Hiding behind an imaginary shield.

7   Using the turtle technique and protecting yourself inside your shell.

8   Taking some exercise – running, football, shooting baskets.

9   Having a special place to go.

10   Having a special person to be with.

11   Listening to music.

12   Breathing deeply and slowly.

13   Relaxing clenched muscles.

The three that I think I will try are:

1   ....

2   ....

3   ....

Other things that I do to help me stay calm are..

....

....

DRAWING THE FEELINGS IN MY BODY

Understanding where we feel strong emotions in our bodies can help us to notice and manage them quickly.

Procedure

1   Ask the child/young person to draw a picture of what is making him/her upset. This does not have to be a good piece of art. Expressing feelings in colours is fine.

2   Draw/copy an outline of a body – you or the child/young person can do this.

3   Ask the child/young person to colour in on the body where he/she feels upset.

4   Ask the child/young person to close their eyes and breathe slowly, smoothly and regularly, six times.

5   Now ask the child/young person to draw something that makes them happy – again colours are fine.

6   Go back to the body outline and ask if the colours on the body feel different.

   If yes:

7   Ask where in their body feels different?

8   Take another body outline and choose new colours for where the body feels different.

9   Ask the child/young person to think about the original incident and say what comes into his/her head about it now. This is usually different from before and is less negative, and new ways of appraising the original incident emerge.

   If no:

Go back to stage 4 and repeat.

Source: Day, J. (2007)

Appendix 11

DEVELOPING A SOLUTION

Think about the last time you became really angry. Answer the following questions about it:

What was the trigger?..

What did you think about the incident?..

What did you do to try to keep calm?...

On a scale of 1 to 10, with 1 being the worst it could possibly be, and 10 being the best, *circle the number* that describes how you feel you reacted.

very badly   *very well*

   1   2   3   4   5   6   7   8   9   10

Assuming you have not circled 1, there must be something about how you behaved that you felt went well. List up to three of those things below.

1   ....

2   ....

3   ....

How could you improve your score by one next time by building on the things that are already going well or by trying new things?

Three things I would do differently next time that would improve my score from .... to ..... are:

1   ....

2   ....

3   ....

Remember, you do not have to be perfect first time; just make some changes that you think would be OK for you. If you find this difficult, talk it through with a trusted adult.

Obstacles

Sometimes when we are trying to make changes, things seem to get in the way and make it difficult for us. List below the things that you think will make it difficult for you to make changes:

....

....

....

How could you avoid these obstacles?..

....

....

....

Who could help you with this?

1   ....

2   ....

3   ....

You have now:

1   Scored your own behaviour on a scale of 1 to 10.

2   Identified what you are doing well already.

3   Decided what you would like to do to improve your score by one.

4   Thought about what might stop you from making those changes.

5   Identified how you could avoid the obstacles and who could help you with this.

You are now ready to put together your own action plan for improving your anger management.

Action plan

The next time I get really angry the **triggers** are likely to be:

1 ....

2 ....

3 ....

I will try to avoid these triggers by:

1 ....

2 ....

3 ....

I will know that I am getting angry because I will notice the **signs**:

....

....

....

I will try to keep **calm** by:

....

....

....

If I cannot avoid the triggers I will **think differently** about them. My thoughts will be:

....

....

....

I will know that my behaviour is better because instead of:

shouting   kicking   throwing things   swearing   damaging things   fighting

other...

(circle the one/s below that fit your behaviour or add your own)

I will: walk away   go to a special place   find someone to talk to

take some exercise   count to ten

other...

I will avoid the obstacles to changing my behaviour by:

....

....

....

The people I will need to help me succeed with this plan are:

1 ....

2 ....

3 ....

Signed _____ Name _____ Date _____

Appendix 12

A SOLUTION-FOCUSED INTERVIEW WITH A YOUNG PERSON PRONE TO ANGRY OUTBURSTS

The process outlined here uses procedures associated with solution-focused approaches. One of these is to 'externalise' the problem, which is a way of looking at the situation so that the youngster sees that he has a relationship to the anger that is viewed as not being 'inside' him, but instead is talked about and labelled as something 'outside' him, which causes difficulties. Another is to ask a 'miracle question' (see Metcalf, 2003).

Initial session

Tell me about the times when this anger takes control over you.	(Identification of triggers and physiological cues?)
Can you give it a name so that we can talk about it?	(Externalisation)
Tell me about the times when you have been able take over and have some control over the anger.	(Putting the fuse out?)
What things will you be able to do when the anger no longer takes control over you? How will your relationships with others change when the anger no longer takes control over you?	(Application of a type of 'miracle' question)

Think of some situations that might happen over the next week when you would like to be in control of the anger.	
How have you managed to gain a bit of control over the anger before?	(Exceptions)
How will this help you over the coming week?	(Identifying strategies that the youngster has been already successful to some extent)
On a scale of 1 (the anger is in total control) to 10 (you are in total control), a) *Where are you now on that scale?* b) *Where would be good enough for you to be at on the scale?* c) *Where would you like to be on the scale next time we meet?*	(Scaling technique)

Review session

Repeat the scaling activity above.

Tell me about the times when you took control.

What did you do differently?

What did others notice?

What effect did this control have on your relationships with others?

Source: Dr. Bob Carabine (Educational Psychologist, Hampshire Educational Psychology Service)

Appendix 13

THE BEGINNINGS OF CHANGE

Change is nearly always difficult because there are both advantages and disadvantages in our present behaviour. Motivational Interviewing recognises and accepts the ambivalence that is usually present. This activity tries to help the young person reflect on the relative importance of the *pulls* to carry on as we are, and the *pushes* into doing things differently. It helps them to identify areas in which to set goals for themselves by rating how anger is affecting their satisfaction in each section of the anger pie on a scale of 1 to 10. A score of 10 (on the edge of the circle) means anger is not affecting anything in this part of their life, whilst a score of 1 (at the centre of the circle) means that this area is being very badly affected by their anger. Join up the scores and you will see where things are a little wobbly!

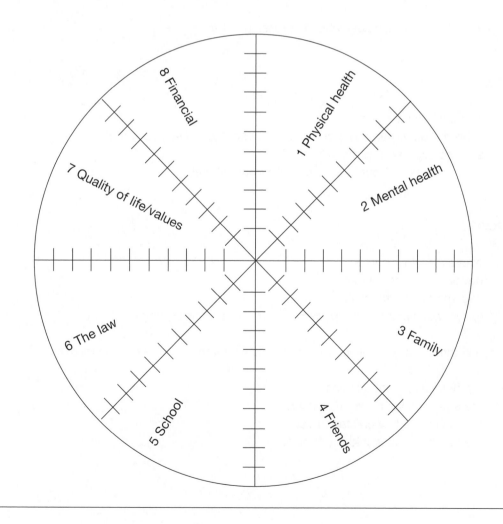

Appendix 14

EFFECTIVE ANGER

The foregoing appendices have helped us to develop the understanding, skills and strategies needed to avoid explosive outbursts of anger that lead to the difficulties associated with problem anger.

The challenge now is how to express anger effectively, in order to provide opportunities to learn and to change. Anger needs to be expressed in a way that respects other people's feelings and points of view, even when they differ from our own. The expression of anger can then be a positive way of resolving conflict and leading to more effective communication between people. In this way, relationships can develop and improve as misunderstandings are resolved over time.

Important issues to consider when expressing anger:

Do:

- wait until you are calm;
- value the other person's point of view, even if you disagree with it;
- express your feelings clearly;
- offer a solution about how it could be done differently.

Don't:

- blame the other person;
- devalue the other person;
- become confrontational;
- exaggerate what has happened (i.e. get it out of proportion).

When communicating feelings to others, it is useful to separate out the following:

- the **behaviour** that has upset you;
- the **effect** on your own behaviour;
- the **feelings** it has created in you;
- the **solution** you would like to see.

For example:

For a pupil:

When people accuse me of deliberately not doing my homework.
(the **behaviour**)

I get a detention.
(the **effect**)

It makes me feel angry because I feel picked on.
(the **feeling**)

I would like to be able to discuss it with you first.
(the **solution**)

For a teacher:

When children shout out.
(the **behaviour**)

It stops me teaching.
(the **effect**)

and makes me feel frustrated and short-tempered.
(the **feeling**)

I would like you to put your hand up.
(the **solution**)

Appendix 15

TIPS FOR PARENTS OF TODDLERS

As children develop from babyhood to their infant years, they have to deal with strong feelings that have not been experienced before. They are developing by exploring, investigating, watching others, imitating, playing with others, and trying out new activities and ideas. There are, however, lots of things they cannot do or are not allowed to do at this stage, which can lead to feelings of confusion and frustration. We often expect children to be grown up one minute ('Be a big girl now...') but babies the next ('You're not old enough to...'). Being bossy and 'in charge' is one way in which we cover up feelings of uncertainty and helplessness.

Anger can sometimes be a way of expressing other emotions, fear, sadness, frustration. Small children can often feel scared about new situations and people. It is important that we try to understand what the purpose of the anger is.

We all need attention from others, but small children need it more than most. It is difficult to switch from getting all the attention a baby gets to being a toddler/young child who is expected to play on their own. Children will get the attention that they need in one way or another. If they do not get it when they are 'good', they will get it by being 'bad'. Playing with small children is an important way to show your interest and love. Allowing them to take control of the play, and for you to do it 'their way', is a safe way for children to feel in control of things.

We have learnt our own ways of expressing anger, and how we feel about our children's anger may well be to do with what happened to us as children. It may be difficult for us to let our children express strong emotions effectively if we were not taught to do this ourselves. Children need us to be able to let them express strong feelings whilst still showing that we can continue to love and take care of them.

Children learn by example more effectively than from words, so it is important to look at our own ways of expressing strong emotions too. The stresses of having a young family can be great. The demands of babies and young children can lead to feelings of insecurity and depression in adults. We must take time to take care of ourselves as well, by getting support from others where possible. If these normal levels of stress are added to by illness, financial worries, bereavement, relationship difficulties etc., we can sometimes be left feeling that we are unable to enjoy our children. It is even more difficult to love an angry toddler when we are having difficulties of our own.

Remember:

Children must learn that being good is the best way to get your attention.

Expressing angry feelings is normal, children need to feel that they can be upset and angry but still be loved and valued.

Taking care of ourselves is important in helping us to take care of our children.

Do:

- give real choices;
- turn the task into a game;
- be honest, even when you think the child won't like it;
- be clear about what is expected;
- give time for settling into new or unknown situations;
- take it seriously if the child is not ready to manage a difficult situation;
- think first – don't react too quickly (unless they are in danger);
- give time for children to discuss things if they are negotiable;
- give clear warnings well in advance (e.g. bedtime in half an hour);
- keep your voice calm;
- avoid battles that are unnecessary;
- be consistent.

Think about:

- Anger is normal – both yours and theirs.
- Sometimes they are feeling muddled and unsure.
- Try to understand what the anger is about – although this is not always easy.
- Anger sometimes covers other feelings, e.g. fear, disappointment, frustration, sadness.
- How does their anger make you feel?
- Do you manage to spend some time with your child most days?
- Does your child get more attention from you when they are being naughty or being good?
- Do you and your partner agree on how to manage your child?
- Discuss disagreements between yourself and your partner when your child isn't there.

This is practice for the teenage years!

Appendix 16

TIPS FOR PARENTS OF PRIMARY AGE CHILDREN

Most children are adaptable and improve their ability to cope with difficult feelings as they mature. For some, however, it seems particularly difficult to tolerate frustration. This may be a result of a number of factors – personality, learnt patterns of behaviour, emotional stresses, illness.

As children get older it is easier to discuss their difficulties with them. It may be that the reasons for angry outbursts can be identified. Recording angry outbursts and looking at when they happen, and who they happen with, may also help us to find out more about what the anger is about.

At primary level, children are continuing to develop their skills through learning both at home and at school. Relationships with siblings and friends become a focus for learning social skills. It is important to encourage children to learn negotiating skills in arguments with friends and family and not to intervene too quickly for them. This will increase their feelings of being in control and managing their own lives successfully.

As children become more able to master new skills effectively, it can sometimes be difficult for them not to expect themselves to get everything 'right' first time. It is important that children learn at this stage that getting things 'wrong' is an important part of learning and does not change their value or worth.

Frustration behaviours can also be seen in children who find if difficult to wait. Children are all individuals and some seem to learn to wait effectively without any difficulty. For others, however, it is a skill that needs to be taught.

It is important not to forget that older children, as well as infants, need to feel secure and loved. Although they seem more independent physically and have not yet reached the pressures of adolescence, they still have emotional needs that we must think carefully about. Children do not want to win all the time, although they give us that impression. In order to feel secure, it is important that the adults in their lives are able to protect them when they feel unable to do so for themselves. Being firm with children is being kind to them, whereas giving in will create unhappy, insecure children. It is important that we provide clear rules for children and that we make them explicit. Children also need us to be consistent where possible in order to be sure that we mean what we say. It is helpful, too, if all the significant adults in the child's life are doing the same things. When schools and families are working together, children have a better chance of changing their behaviour. They also feel secure and confident in the knowledge that all important adults think broadly the same way.

As children mature, they are still using adult role models, so we have a perfect opportunity to show children how to express anger in a non-destructive way, by being calm and assertive. It may be appropriate to ignore the child's angry outburst, but only if you feel that it will not escalate the behaviour and it is safe to do so. It is important to ensure that you are giving plenty of attention when the child is being good. This is not always easy as we are inclined to feel that we can get on with other things when the child is playing/working well. Recognising good behaviour with praise, a cuddle or a treat later in the day is very effective, however.

When punishment is needed, it is important that it is timely, appropriate and clear what it is for, in order that the child understands what they have done wrong. The severity of the punishment is far less important than the consistency with which it is applied. It is also important to help the child maintain their self-esteem by making it clear that it is the behaviour that is inappropriate and not that the child themselves are 'bad' in some way.

Do:

- allow children to sort out their own battles, where safe to do so, but keep an ear open;
- wait until you are both calm before you sit down and talk about the angry outbursts;
- teach your child to ask for help with difficult tasks, before frustration sets in;
- ignore mild anger if it will not escalate, and is safe to do so;
- allow children to make mistakes and help them to learn from them;
- help children to learn to wait;
- stay calm – demonstrate ways of expressing anger that are not destructive.

Think about

- labelling the *behaviour* you do not like as inappropriate, rather than the child;
- providing a consistent approach to dealing with difficult behaviours. Schools and family can support each other by ensuring a consistent approach across all situations. Teachers, special needs assistants, lunchtime supervisors and parents should all be working together to provide consistent messages, rewards and sanctions;
- Sometimes it is more effective to provide small rewards for good behaviour than to punish inappropriate behaviour, but this is only likely to be true when behaviours can be safely ignored. When punishment is needed it will be most effective when it is:
  - clearly associated with the behaviour you want to change;
  - close to the event;
  - consistently applied – research has shown that punishment does not have to be severe to be effective, but it must be the same each time the behaviour occurs.

Giving some special time to children when you are sharing a task, without criticism or judgement, is very effective in helping children feel valued and emotionally secure.

Appendix 17

TIPS FOR PARENTS OF TEENAGERS

It is difficult for us to realise that children have developed into young adults and to change our behaviour accordingly. Adolescents are coping with a number of conflicting pressures, success at school/exams, finding an adult identity, maintaining peer relationships, developing sexuality. It is normal for adolescents to push against the boundaries that are set, as they want to take control of themselves and their lives. Adolescents have strong emotional needs, however, and the conflicting pressures make it even more important that they feel secure in their usual/known environments, e.g. school/home.

Although we can explain difficult adolescent behaviours by looking at external and internal conflicts, this is not a reason for condoning inappropriate behaviours. Adolescents need the boundaries we set for them in order for them to feel safe. It is important, however, that they are moving towards self-management and setting their own boundaries as well. Negotiation and compromise are therefore important aspects of relationships between adults and adolescents.

Adolescents are very concerned about 'fairness', so it is important to be consistent in our responses and to discuss our reasons for the limits we are imposing. Young peoples' feelings of needing to belong to a group are very strong at this stage. They will need to belong to a group of friends, but also need to feel they belong at home.

Teenagers often give us the impression that their group of friends is more important than their families. This is an outward expression of the conflict of becoming independent, whilst still needing emotional support and guidance. It is equally important at this stage that young people know that they are loved and cared for at home.

Teenagers are good at pushing our emotional buttons. If we get upset and over-emotional it is more difficult for us to think effectively and solve problems calmly. Don't be tempted to call them names or threaten them with throwing them out. Getting angry does not help us solve the problem or help our relationships, and may lead to punishments that are out of proportion. Young people will learn effective ways of resolving conflicts by example as well as by negotiation.

Living with teenagers can be a difficult and stressful time. We are also having to make the transition from our role as full-time parents to people who have our own lives to lead. This, in itself, can be a difficult transition for parents. It is important that we take care of ourselves if we are to be good role models for our children and help them learn effective ways of expressing their angry feelings.

Do:

- listen to their point of view;
- value their point of view, even when you do not agree with it;
- respond calmly when explaining your point of view;
- have clear rules, rewards and sanctions;
- make boundaries explicit and clear;
- explain the reasons for your rules;
- negotiate rules together where possible and safe – but be clear when negotiation is not an option;
- aim for a win/win solution;
- wait until you are both calm to discuss things;
- avoid disciplining in anger;
- avoid making promises/threats that you cannot carry out;
- aim to enforce rules consistently.

Think about:

- Although angry outbursts may be directed at you personally, it is helpful to de-personalise them by understanding that you are being asked to provide a boundary. The conflict is probably not between two people but between the young person and authority.
- A major source of conflict between people is poor communication – misunderstanding about intentions, motives etc. can affect the way we respond. It is important to check that we have understood the young person's point of view and that they have understood ours.
- It is very easy to think they must know what you are thinking or feeling, particularly if you know someone well. It is often necessary to be explicit however, and not make the mistake of thinking that they must know what you mean without checking it out.
- It is important to check that there are no extra stresses contributing to the behaviour, e.g. bullying, school work, peer pressure.
- Adolescents are experts at bringing 'red herrings' into an argument. We may find ourselves being taken down an irrelevant track rather than continuing with the request in hand. It may be helpful to employ the broken record technique:

    Parent: *'Would you tidy your room before you go out please?'*

    Teenager: *'I did it yesterday.'*

    Parent: *'Would you tidy your room before you go out please?'*

    Teenager: *'You haven't asked [Jane] to tidy her room!'*

    Parent: *'Please would you to tidy your room before you go out?!'*

- It is very tempting for us to get drawn into a discussion about other issues rather than staying on track. When you are being appropriately assertive, most young people will respond, albeit grudgingly.
- Learning to express strong feelings effectively now will be good grounding for adult life.

Appendix 18

WHAT CHILDREN AND TEACHERS SAY ABOUT ANGER

1. What children say about anger

Children from three different schools were asked:

- What makes you angry?
- What happens when you get angry at home?
- What happens when you get angry at school?
- How do you control your anger?

The children's responses, which follow, give some first-hand insight into what children think about anger.

What makes you angry?

- When other children kick me.
- When other girls talk about me behind my back.
- When my friend doesn't play with me.
- When no-one passes to me in football.
- When I get sums wrong.
- When things take a long time.
- I just do!
- When other people get hurt.
- When I think of hungry/starving children.
- When I don't get enough food.
- When my parents have a 'favourite' in the family.
- When my baby brother gets all the attention.
- When I didn't do anything.
- When the others were doing it as well.
- 'cause she doesn't like me.
- 'cause my mum says I'm going to another school.
- 'cause my mum says you're rubbish.
- When dad throws my toys away.

- When my friend says I can't play.
- When my mum shouts at me to get my coat on.
- Some boys throwing berries at me and I didn't do anything to them.
- The boys who climb up the trees and look in my house.
- When people touch my dinner.
- When someone is beating me at football.
- When someone is nasty to my friends.
- When someone joins in my game without asking.
- When mum shouts.
- When mum doesn't let me watch television.
- When my little sister makes a mess and I have to tidy it up.
- My brother when he pinches my toys/sister gets in my bed/brother kicks me/ climbs on me/spoils my model/spoils my things.
- When someone hurts me.
- When I can't do something or get something to work.
- When someone stops me doing or having what I want.
- When someone gets angry with me.
- When someone bullies me.

What happens when you get angry at home?

- I get smacked.
- I get the strap/belt.
- I get sent to bed early.
- I lose my pocket money.
- I have my toys taken away from me.
- Mum shouts.
- Mum says I'll get put in a home.
- She does nothing.
- She answers a different question.
- Say I'm going to live with my dad.
- I tell mum/dad/nan. Punch them/yell at them.
- I smack my dad back.
- I kick the furniture.
- I feel like kicking the door down.
- I shout at the people who make me angry.
- I run around to make me feel better.
- I go away and ignore the person that annoyed me.
- I go to my room and stop talking to mum.
- I call them names and throw mud at them.
- Sometimes I shout.
- I go off and find another friend.
- I tell a dinner lady/teacher. (Don't shout at school or hit out; its dangerous/you get told off.)
- I refuse to eat.
- I go to my room.

What happens when you get angry at school?

- I hit people.
- I'm rude and use bad words.
- I don't talk to anyone.
- I get told off.
- I get detention.
- I get put on a 'step'.
- I get suspended.
- I do nothing.
- I grind teeth, yell or scream, stamp feet, cry.

How do you control your anger?

- I count to 10.
- I breathe deep.
- I run.
- I shout.
- I say a word that's not rude.
- I go and be quiet.
- I get time out.
- I go to the head teacher.
- I drink some water.
- I think of something that makes me happy.
- I have a lie down and rest.
- I go and play on my own – return when I'm feeling better.
- I give mum a kiss and do as she says.
- I tell my mummy about it.
- I sit down quietly.
- I lie on my bed.
- I go to the shop (forget about it)/Go to the Elephant and Castle (go down the slide there)/Have a cuddle/sweets/treat.
- I tell someone what's made me angry (but they don't always listen).

2. What teachers say about anger

The same questions were also posed to a group of teachers as a prelude to some in-service training on anger management. Their responses are given below. How would you answer these questions?

What makes you angry at work?

- Being asked to do things at very short notice. Being shouted at by staff (not pupils).
- Children – ignored. Staff – not being considered.
- Frustrations regarding time. Working under inconsistent circumstances.

- Pupils mistreating an instrument.
- Pupils who are rude and mouthy.
- Other people not taking responsibility for their bits. Not completing tasks on time. Criticism.
- Being behind with paperwork – being moaned at for having a messy desk.
- People who insult others or myself. Students who show no respect to colleagues or the environment or the work that is going on.
- People not listening to me. People assuming things before asking. People not doing what I tell them.
- Children who refuse point-blank to do what I ask. Rudeness – swearing, challenging requests. Lack of effort – refusal to try.
- Pupils that are deliberately argumentative. Staff asking for work that I see as unnecessary.
- Forced to enforce unenforceable rules. Absences – lack of continuity.
- People letting you down – pupil not bringing in books/work/homework essential to the lesson. Fellow teachers who do not produce work/do items which they should do by required time. Silly behaviour.
- Pupils' deliberate 'winding-up' tactics.
- Being put under unnecessary pressure. Not being able to realise my potential due to inflexible management.
- When I have to backtrack and rework what has been done before.

What makes you angry at home?

- Things like banging my head on a shelf.
- Not being considered.
- Not having enough time to achieve goals. Promises not kept by others.
- My partner not helping with the housework.
- My partner sulking.
- Being let down by others, especially friends and family being late when we are going out.
- When there is something that doesn't work, e.g. hot water, heating. When there is no food left.
- People assuming I'll do things before asking me. People wanting my time!
- Pig-headedness. Systematic attempts to wind me up by people who recognise that they are doing so and labour the point. A dirty/untidy house caused by housemates who then wish me to clean it up. A refusal to understand that I am busy/stressed and *can't* socialise with friends during the week. People who waste my time.
- Poor drivers (sometimes). Not a lot!
- Someone not understanding the demands of my job.
- Partner not doing fair share of housekeeping.
- Rarely angry, more frustrated when there seems to be too many things to cope with. Can get angry when family make me late.
- Children not doing something when asked. When equipment goes wrong.
- When my son leaves his dinner plate on the floor and hasn't picked it up 24 hours later!

What happens when you get angry?

- Nothing much, usually.
- Stubborn – quiet.
- Analyse and change what can be changed. Talk through and compromise where possible. Accept with shrug that which I cannot affect.
- I want to shout lots.
- At school – with students – calm broken record. With staff, stop, listen. Explode in private. At home – try to explain – shout – plot revenge!
- Try to keep it in. Get all tense and irritable. Usually take it out on the wrong person when eventually it comes out.
- I will become silent and think about it. If I am pushed too far I will shout.
- I tend to get caught up in a situation. Physically or verbally show others around me how I am feeling. Tend to make a situation worse.
- Shouting, single out a pupil and tell them their behaviour is unacceptable. Have child removed from room (in extreme circumstances). Home – pointed/nasty comments – personal nasty comments – complete raging behaviour (very occasionally) in which I will scream at someone until I am hoarse and even strike out at them physically. Slamming doors, etc. Throwing things.
- Sometimes I shout, increased body tension.
- Tendency to shout.
- My voice raises.
- At work: give pupil punishment (order or detention) or apply appropriate sanction. Imperative that I don't lose my temper. At home: shout!
- Shout, snap at people.
- I usually go very quiet and walk away. If prompted I become sarcastic.

What do you do to control your anger?

- Let off steam to someone (personally) close to me – not physically close. Rationalise it – think it over and realise it's rather silly to get angry about these things.
- Repress it – in some cases try to justify other person's position to defuse.
- Think.
- Say in my head what I know I *can't* say to the kids. If I'm less stressed I get less angry.
- Physically stop, pause, breathe deeply, rationalise why, talk to others, swim, drink red wine!
- Try to talk it through in my own mind – reason, etc. Calm myself down – sometimes has opposite effect. At home: go for a run or go to the gym.
- Talk about it with someone independent of situation.
- Try (and fail) to calm down. Try (and fail) to stand back from a situation.
- Work: step into role, take a step back from the situation, lower my voice, take a deep breath, rational response to what someone is doing to irritate me. Home: leave the room/situation that is bugging me. Exercise – go for a walk or run.
- Exercise to relieve tension. Think about how I can defuse the situation. Try to put it into context. Walk the dog.
- Slow myself down. Slow my pace.
- Take a deep breath and bite my tongue.

- At work: try to step back from the situation – see whole class. Perhaps ignore source of anger for moment. At home: reason, calm down, start again.
- Consciously take a moment to calm; focus on what really matters.
- I usually wink at the kids and make them laugh. I apologise to adults even though I may be right.

What do you do to control your children's anger?

- Put my toddler in her cot and go and talk to her in five minutes. Older children –send them out to calm down. Walk away from them. Talk to them afterwards. Make a little joke with them.
- Drop into 'immovable object' role.
- Talk, rationalise, calm, discuss.
- Send them out to cool off. Settle them elsewhere to work. Send them to another member of staff.
- Listen – don't confront, defuse – negotiate, delaying tactics, remove audience, suggest practical solutions, build trust.
- Try to encourage to talk. Let them be angry – able to do this during home visit. Give space and time.
- Ask them why they are angry – give them cool off time.
- Try and remove them from one situation. Try to calm them down.
- Lower my voice, ask them to calm down, deep breath, tell me in a sensible way what is making them so cross. If possible, separate the child from the troublesome situation.
- Try to defuse the situation by talking softly, but being firm.
- Try assertive discipline. Try to know them and find a way to avoid them feeling and demonstrating their anger.
- Talk quietly and calmly to them in the hope that it rubs off.
- At work: sometimes giving them space and time to calm down helps, then talk. At home: listen to source of grievance.
- Listen, take time to let them get rid of anger.
- I talk them out of it. Get them to speak slowly and quietly – when calm, talk through the situation. Attempt to transcend their self-centred view.

BIBLIOGRAPHY

Baginsky, W. (undated) *Peer Mediation in the UK: A Guide for Schools*. London: NSPCC Publications and Information Unit.

Beck, A. T. (1988) *Love is Never Enough*. New York: Harper & Row.

Bennathan, M. and Boxall, M. (2000) *Intervention in Primary School: Nurture Groups*, 2nd edn. London: David Fulton Publishers.

Bowlby, J. (1978) *Attachment and Loss*. Harmondsworth: Penguin.

Boxall, M. and Lucas, S. (2010) *Nurture Groups in Schools: Principles and Practice*, 2nd edn. London: Sage Publications.

Breakwell, G. M. (1997) *Coping with Aggressive Behaviour*. Leicester: British Psychological Society.

Brett, D. (1986) *Annie Stories: A Special Kind of Story Telling*. New York: Workman Publishing.

Brett, D. (1992) *More Annie Stories*. New York: Imagination Press.

Bronfenbrenner, U. (1979) *The Ecology of Human Development: Experiments by Nature and Design*. Cambridge, MA: Harvard University Press.

Brown, J. (1967) *Freud and the Post Freudians*. Harmondsworth: Penguin.

Cole, P. M., Martin, S. E. and Dennis, T. A. (2004) 'Emotion regulation as a scientific construct: methodological challenges and directions for child development research'. *Child Development*, 75, 317–33.

Cooper, P. and Tilknaz, T. (2007) *Nurture Groups in School and at Home: Connecting with Children with Social, Emotional and Behavioural Difficulties*. London: Jessica Kingsley Publishers.

Cooper, P. and Cefai, C. (2009) 'Contemporary values and social context: implications for the emotional wellbeing of children'. *Emotional and Behavioural Difficulties*, 14, 2: 91–100.

Cremin, H. (2007) *Peer Mediation: Citizenship and Social Inclusion Revisited*. Maidenhead: McGraw-Hill (for Open University Press).

Crick, N. R. and Dodge, K. A. (2004) 'A review and reformulation of social information-processing mechanisms in children's social adjustment', in R. Kail (ed.), *Children and their Development*. New York: Prentice-Hall.

Damasio, A. (2000) *The Feeling of What Happens: Body, Emotion and the Making of Consciousness.* London: Vintage Books.

Damasio, A. (2003) *Looking for Spinoza: Joy, Sorrow and the Feeling Brain.* New York: Harcourt.

Davis, W. and Frude, N. (1995) *Preventing Face to Face Violence: Dealing with Anger and Aggression at Work*. Thurnby: The Assoociation for Psychological Therapies.

Day, J. (1994) *Creative Visualization with Children: A Practical Guide*. London: Thorsons.

Day, J. (2007) *Being What You Want to See: Bringing Emotional Mastery into Everyday Life*. San Francisco: CA: Shinnyo-en Foundation.

DCSF (2005) *Social and Emotional Aspects of Learning (SEAL)*. London: Department for Children, Schools and Families.

DCSF (2006) *The Use of Force to Control or Restrain Pupils*. London: Department for Children, Schools and Families.

DCSF (2009) *Your Child Your Schools, Our Future*. H.M. Government white paper Cm. 7669. London: The Stationery Office.

DFE (1994) *Code of Practice on the Identification and Assessment of Special Educational Needs*. London: Department for Education.

DfES (2005) *Every Child Matters*. London: Department for Education and Skills.

Dodge, K. A. (1986) 'A social information processing model of social competence in children', in Perlmutter, M. (ed.) *Cognitive Perspectives on Children's Social and Behavioural Development*. Hillsdale, NJ: Lawrence Erlbaum, pp. 77–133.

Dryden, W. (1996) *Overcoming Anger*. London: Sheldon Press.

Ellis, A. and Dryden, W. (1999) *The Practice of Rational Emotive Behavioural Therapy*. New York: Springer.

Erikson, E. (1950) *Childhood and Society*. New York: W.W. Norton.

Faupel, A., Herrick, E. and Sharp, P. (1998) *Anger Management*, 1st edn. London: David Fulton Publishers.

Faupel, A. W. (ed.) (2003) *Emotional Literacy: Assessment and Intervention*. London: nferNELSON.

Feindler, E. and Ecton, R. (1986) *Adolescent Anger Control: Cognitive-behavioral Techniques*. Oxford: Pergamon Press.

Gardner, F. (2006) *Blood and Sand*. London: Transworld Publishers.

Gardner, H. (1993) *Multiple Intelligences: The Theory in Practce*. New York: Basic Books.

Glasser, W. (1986) *Control Theory in the Classroom*. New York: Harper and Row.

Goleman, D. (1996) *Emotional Intelligence: Why It Can Matter more than IQ*. London: Bloomsbury.

Gordon, T. (2003) *Teacher Effectiveness Training*. New York: Three Rivers Press.

Harris, T. A. (2004) I'm OK, You're OK. New York: Harper Paperbacks.

HM Government (2009) *Building Britain's Future*. London: The Stationery Office. Cm. 7654.

Hopkins, B. (2004) *Just Schools: A Whole School Approach to Restorative Justice*. London: Jessica Kingsley Publishers.

House of Commons Health Committee (2003) *The Victoria Climbié Inquiry Report*. London: The Stationery Office.

Kohn, A. (1999) *Punished by Rewards: The Trouble with Gold Stars, Incentive Plans, A's, Praise, and Other Bribes*. Boston MA: Houghton Mifflin.

Laming, L. (2009) *The Protection of Children in England: A Progress Report*. London: The Stationery Office.

Layard, R. and Dunn, J. (2009) *A Good Childhood: Searching for Values in a Competitive Age*. London: Penguin.

LeDoux, J. (1994) 'Emotion, memory and the brain'. *Scientific American*, 270, 6: 50–7.

LeDoux, J. (1998) *The Emotional Brain: The Mysterious Underpinnings of Emotional Life*. New York: Simon and Schuster.

Lewin, K. (1936) *Principles of Topological Psychology*. New York: McGraw-Hill.

Lyubomirsky, S. (2007) *The How of Happiness*. London: Sphere.

McNamara, E. (1998) *Motivational Interviewing*. Ainsdale: Positive Behaviour Management.

McNamara, E. (ed.) (2009) *Motivational Interviewing: Theory, Practice and Applications with Children and Young People*. Ainsdale: Positive Behaviour Management.

Maslow, A. H. (1943) 'A theory of human motivation.' *Psychological Review*, 50: 370–96.

Maslow, A. H. (1968) *Towards a Psychology of Being*. New York: Van Nostrand.

Metcalf, L. (2003) *Teaching Toward Solutions*. Carmarthen: Crown House Publishing.

National Commission on Education (1996) *Success Against the Odds: Effective Schools in Disadvantaged Areas*. London: Routledge.

Patterson, G. (1986) 'Performance models for antisocial boys'. *American Psychologist*, 41: 432–44.

Potter-Efron, R. (2005) *Angry all the Time: An Emergency Guide to Anger Control*. Oakland, CA: New Harbinger Publications.

Segal, J. (1992) *Melanie Klein*. London: Sage.

Seligman, M. E. P. (2002) 'Positive psychology, positive prevention and positive therapy', in Snyder, C. R. and Lopez, S. J. *Handbook of Positive Psychology*. Oxford: Oxford University Press.

Shapiro, L. (1994) *The Anger Control Kit*. Indiana, PA: Center for Applied Psychology.

Sharp, P. and Herrick, E. (2000) 'Promoting emotional literacy: anger management groups', in Barwick, N. *Clinical Counselling in Schools*. London: Routledge.

Spence, S. (1995) *Social Skills Training: Enhancing Social Competence with Children and Adults*. London: NferNelson.

Stallard, P. (2005) *A Clinician's Guide to Think Good – Feel Good: The Use of CBT with Children and Young People*. Chichester: John Wiley.

Steer, Sir A. (2005) *Learning Behaviour. The Report of the Practitioners' Group on School Behaviour and Discipline*. Nottingham: DfES.

Steer, Sir A. (2009) *Learning Behaviour – Lessons Learned: A Review of Behaviour Standards and Practices in our Schools*. Nottingham: DCSF.

Ury, W. and Fisher, R. (1991) *Getting to Yes: Negotiating Agreement without Giving In*. Harmondsworth: Penguin.

Waters, T. (2004) *Therapeutic Storywriting: A Practical Guide to Developing Emotional Literacy in Primary Schools*. London: David Fulton Publishers.

Watkins, A. (1997) *Mind-Body Medicine: A Clinician's Guide to Psychoneuroimmunology*. Oxford: Churchill-Livingstone.

Woodcock, C. (in press) *Group Work with Angry Children*. London: Routledge.

Zohar, D. and Marshall, I. N. (2004) *Spiritual Capital: Wealth We Can Live by*. San Francisco, CA: Berrett-Koehler.

INDEX

A Good Childhood xi
ABC Model 11
Amygdala 26
Anger expressed effectively (normal anger) 29
Anger spoilers 52, 64
Anger triggers 29, 91, 63, 64, 80, 89, 94, 96
Angry log 64, 95, 96
Angry thermometer 64, 94, 95
Aristotle 5
Assault Cycle 6–7, 57–60, 63, 69, 70–3
Assertiveness 46, 49, 80, 115, 117
Attachment Theory xiv, 4, 13

Behaviour log 53
Behaviour modification 50, 53, 84
Behaviourist Approaches 10–12
Belief systems 25, 29
Bowlby, John 13
Breakwell, Glenys 6
Bronfenbrenner's ecological model 34

Calming techniques 65, 69, 70, 71, 73
CASEL 12
Children's Workforce Development Council x
Classroom and group management 22, 36, 44
Cognitive Behavioural approaches 14–15, 25, 64, 66, 84
Cognitive restructuring 65–6
Cohesiveness 44
Common Assessment Framework (CAF) x
Communication 29, 38, 46, 49–50, 62, 70, 117
Conduct disorders 83

Conflict resolution 52
Conflict resolution 52, 79
Confrontation 38, 44, 82
Constancy 43
Cortisol 20, 21
Crisis management 4, 69

Debriefing 69, 74
Defusing techniques 45, 56, 57 61, 63, 67
Distraction 61–3
Dodge, Kenneth 15

Early warning signs 56, 57, 59
Ecological Model 34
Effective anger 110
Ellis, Albert 14, 25
Empathy 7, 37, 44, 45, 58
Erikson, Erik 88, 89
Every Child Matters ix, 4

Feindler and Ecton 6
Firework Model 5–10, 14, 58
Freud, Sigmund 12–13
Friendships 22

Gardner, Frank 14
Gardner, Richard 84
Glasser, William 3, 63
Goleman 2, 3, 5, 27

Handling crises 39
Humour 61, 62

I-Messages 29, 50, 52
Instrumental anger 18

Keeping calm 109–10

Klein, Melanie 86

Laming Report ix
Lead Professional x
Learned responses 25
Levels of intervention 35–6

Managing feelings 44
Maslow 3, 4, 16, 26
Maslow's hierarchy 4, 16, 38
McNamara, E. 82
Mediation 79
Mental health 4, 19, 22, 109
Motivation 12, 37, 44, 45, 82
Motivational Interviewing 81, 82, 109

Novaco, R. 5

Observation Checklist – Primary 92
Observation Checklist – Secondary 93

Parents and primary age children 114–5
Parents and teenagers 116–7
Parents and toddlers, 112–3
Peer mediation 37, 79
Personal anger pie 19
Physical health 19, 27, 109
Physical intervention 68, 71, 73–5
Physical proximity 51, 61, 62
Problem anger 77, 83, 84, 90
Prochaska, J. A. and DiClemente, C. 82
Psychodynamic Approaches 12, 13, 26,
    27, 83

Relaxation 62, 63, 65, 82, 83
Relocation 61, 62
Repressed anger 27, 28, 32

Restorative Justice 78–9
Rewards and sanctions 11–13, 37, 38,
    42, 44, 72, 84
Risk assessment 74

School Behaviour policy 36–40
SEAL xiii, 36
Self talk and calming techniques 65, 84
Self-actualisation 4
Self-awareness 27, 44
Self-esteem xiii, 12, 13, 26, 27, 37, 42,
    46, 50, 53, 58, 61, 62, 71, 89, 90, 96,
    115
Social skills xiii, 12, 16, 37, 38, 39, 44,
    45–6, *51*, 80, 1 112
Solution Focused Approaches 80–1, 84,
    104–8
Stages of childhood 88
Stallard, Paul 66
Steer Report x, 36
Suppressed anger 28
Sure Start x

Tavistock clinic 84
Teaching good behaviour 11, 37, 39, 44,
    52–3
Therapeutic stories/metaphors 82–4

Unconscious motivators 25, 26, 27, 83

Voltaire 29

Whole school environment 37
Whole school factors 36, 43

You-Messages, 29